Glimpsing the Future

Glimpsing the Future

New Testament Perspectives on Death, Resurrection,
Immortality, Eternity, and the Afterlife

Murray J. Harris

CASCADE *Books* · Eugene, Oregon

GLIMPSING THE FUTURE
New Testament Perspectives on Death, Resurrection, Immortality, Eternity, and the Afterlife

Cascade Books
An Imprint of Wipf and Stock Publishers
199 W. 8th Ave., Suite 3
Eugene, OR 97401

www.wipfandstock.com

PAPERBACK ISBN: 979-8-3852-2726-6
HARDCOVER ISBN: 979-8-3852-2727-3
EBOOK ISBN: 979-8-3852-2728-0

Cataloguing-in-Publication data:

Names: Harris, Murray J. [author].
Title: Glimpsing the future : New Testament perspectives on death, resurrection, immortality, eternity, and the afterlife / by Murray J. Harris.
Description: Eugene, OR: Cascade Books, 2024 | Includes bibliographical references.
Identifiers: ISBN 979-8-3852-2726-6 (paperback) | ISBN 979-8-3852-2727-3 (hardcover) | ISBN 979-8-3852-2728-0 (ebook)
Subjects: LCSH: Eschatology—Biblical teaching. | Resurrection—Biblical teaching. | Immortality—Biblical teaching. | Death—Biblical teaching. | Eternity.
Classification: BS2545.R47 H377 2024 (paperback) | BS2545.R47 (ebook)

VERSION NUMBER 09/20/24

To David Burt and Dr. Graham D. Smith

sterling and stimulating friends
for eighty years

Contents

Preface

ACCOUNTS OF "NEAR DEATH" experiences and visits to heaven, so readily available on the internet, are common fare for anyone inquisitive about the afterlife. Why, then, yet another book that explores this topic of perennial interest?

What I have endeavored to do in this relatively short book that is free of footnotes is to provide a "convenient summary" of the teaching of the New Testament about death and the afterlife. Rightly or wrongly, I see my approach as being distinctive in several regards.

- There is an examination of the personal encounters of Jesus, Paul, and Peter with death as the background for their teaching about death.

- I trace the meanings of all the crucial Greek words found in the New Testament that describe aspects of death and the life to come.

- I outline in detail the arguments proposed in defense of the historical resurrection of Jesus from the dead, and then state and seek to answer some nine objections that are often raised against belief in his resurrection.

- Throughout the history of Christian thought there has been a tendency to drive a wedge between the concepts of resurrection and immortality. I have tried to demonstrate that these two concepts, so far from being mutually exclusive, are in fact both inseparable and complementary ideas that reflect unambiguous New Testament thought. There is a detailed comparison of Plato's and Paul's view on immortality.

- There is a detailed discussion of the character of the "spiritual body."

- How the New Testament struggles to express the concept of eternity is examined.

- Heaven as the abode of the righteous in the intermediate and final states is defended.

- Contentious issues such as Hades, purgatory, hell, annihilationism, universalism, and the nature of the new heavens and new earth are briefly addressed.

Whether the author has been in any way successful in communicating these distinctives is for the reader to decide.

Acknowledgments

Two publishers (Eerdmans and Zondervan) have kindly given permission to reproduce, usually with changes, material that first appeared in books I authored: *Raised Immortal: Resurrection and Immortality in the New Testament* (Grand Rapids: Eerdmans, 1985); *From Grave to Glory: Resurrection in the New Testament* (Grand Rapids: Zondervan, 1990); *Prepositions and Theology in the Greek New Testament* (Grand Rapids: Zondervan, 2012).

Few authors have the privilege that I have to express warm gratitude to two stalwart and treasured friends of eighty years, Dr. Graham D. Smith and David Burt, who once again have read and helpfully commented on my manuscript. It is my consummate pleasure to dedicate the present volume to them.

Also, I am grateful to my wife, Lynette, for her patient encouragement of an octogenarian during recent months.

All translations of ancient texts are my own.

Abbreviations

AD	*Anno Domini* (Latin), "in the year of our Lord" (= the Christian era)
BC	Before Christ
BDAG	*A Greek-English Lexicon of the New Testament and Other Early Christian Literature* (rev. and ed. Frederick W. Danker; Chicago/London: University of Chicago, 2000), based on Walter Bauer's *Griechisch-deutsches Wörterbuch* (6th ed.) and on previous English eds. by W. F. Arndt, F. W. Gingrich, and F. W. Danker
	References are given by page number and by a–d (= the four sections of the page)
Bruce, *Acts*	F. F. Bruce, *The Book of Acts* (Grand Rapids: Eerdmans, 1988)
c.	*circa* (Latin), about
cf.	*confer* (Latin), compare
d.	died
EVV	English versions of the New Testament
Harris, *2 Cor*	M. J. Harris, *The Second Epistle to the Corinthians: A Commentary on the Greek Text,*

	ed. I. H. Marshall and D. A. Hagner (Grand Rapids: Eerdmans/Milton Keyes: Paternoster, 2005)
Harris, *Immortality*	M. J. Harris, *Raised Immortal: Resurrection and Immortality in the New Testament* (London: Marshall, Morgan & Scott, 1983/ Grand Rapids: Eerdmans, 1985)
Harris, *Prepositions*	M. J. Harris, *Prepositions and Theology in the Greek New Testament* (Grand Rapids: Zondervan, 2012)
Harris, *Questions*	M. J. Harris, *Three Crucial Questions about Jesus* (Grand Rapids: Baker, 1994/Eugene, Oregon: Wipf & Stock, 2008)
Harris, *Resurrection*	M. J. Harris, *From Grave to Glory: Resurrection in the New Testament* (Grand Rapids: Zondervan 1990)
Harris, *Slave*	M. J. Harris, *Slave of Christ: A New Testament Metaphor for Total Devotion to Christ* (Leicester: Apollos/Downers Grove, Illinois: InterVarsity, 1999)
Harris, *Texts (1)*	M. J. Harris, *Navigating Tough Texts: A Guide to Problem Passages in the New Testament. Volume 1* (Bellingham, Washington: Lexham, 2020)
Harris, *Texts (2)*	M. J. Harris, *Navigating Tough Texts: A Guide to Problem Passages in the New Testament. Volume 2* (Bellingham, Washington: Lexham, 2024)
JSOT	Journal for the Study of the Old Testament
LSB	Legacy Standard Bible (updated NASB) (2021)

LSJ	H. G. Liddell and R. Scott, *A Greek-English Lexicon* (9th ed.; rev. H. S. Jones et al.; Oxford: Clarendon, 1940). *Supplement* (ed. E. A. Barber et al. Oxford: Clarendon, 1968)
LXX	Septuagint (= Greek Old Testament)
NASB	New American Standard Bible (1999)
NIDNTT	*The New International Dictionary of New Testament Theology,* 3 vols., ed. Colin Brown (Grand Rapids: Zondervan, 1975–78)
NIV	New International Version (2011)
NRSV	New Revised Standard Version Bible (1989)
NT	New Testament
OT	Old Testament
passim	(Latin) in many places
RSV	Revised Standard Version (1952)

I. Death and the Afterlife in Pre-Christian Thought

A. *Egyptian Concepts*

We are dependent on three main sources for our knowledge of ancient Egyptian views of death and the afterlife.

1. The Pyramid Texts reflect views of the Old Kingdom period (2800–2500 BC). Originally they described the destiny of the pharaohs alone, but they came to depict the fate of ordinary people. The deceased person traveled to the underworld in the far West where the "great god" Osiris, the god of vegetation and regeneration, reigned. What Egyptians feared was not the benevolent Osiris who became incarnate in every pharaoh but the judgmental Osiris who as lord of the underworld determined the destiny of the souls of the dead. The same basic pattern of ritual magical rites was practiced for almost three thousand years, down to the fourth century AD. Prayers for the dead were addressed to Ra, the chief of the gods and the primary god of the sun, as well as to Osiris, seeking for the dead to be mystically identified with the divine Osiris and to be absorbed into the rhythm of the universe. But such transformation required that the dead be preserved from physical disintegration—hence the elaborate procedure known as "mummification," a technique of

---

* What follows under A–B, D is a summary of Harris, *Resurrection*, 31–79 (used with permission).

embalming carried out for almost three thousand years (c. 2600 BC—AD 300). Even after this physical protection from the ravages of time, mummies were placed in coffins and in tombs. Before a mummy was placed in one of these "houses of eternity," the officiating priest would perform a magical ceremony called "the Opening of the Mouth," touching the eyes, nostrils, and mouth to restore the dead person's ability to see, breathe, and receive food.

2. The Coffin Texts of the Middle Kingdom (2134–1786 BC) are a collection of over eleven hundred funerary spells written on coffins or sometimes on tomb walls. Whereas the Pyramid Texts focused on the celestial realm, the Coffin Texts focused on the subterranean region where the spells of these texts protected the dead from the dangers of this realm and a "second death."

3. The Book of the Dead, dating in its earliest form from the Old Kingdom (Fifth Dynasty, c. 2600 BC). Both the Coffin Texts and this Book of the Dead describe postmortem judgment. The dead person is brought by the jackal-headed mortuary god Anubis into the great Hall of the Two Truths and is set before Osiris, the Lord of Eternity, who is seated on his throne with Isis and Nephthys in attendance. The fateful verdict is given and recorded by the divine scribe Thoth, Master of the Balance. If the dead person's heart is right before Maat, god of Truth or Justice, they are allowed to enter the Osirian Fields in the West. If not, they are devoured by Ammut, "the eater of the dead."

But an Osirian view of the hereafter was the dominant outlook in ancient Egypt. When a person was preserved physically by mummification and the magical mortuary rites were performed, their personality or "soul" (*ka*) would be changed into a superhuman being (*akh*) and assume various forms, become united with Osiris, and continue to enjoy earthly pleasures in Duat, "the abode of those who are faultless."

B. Greek Concepts

We may identify four stages in the development of the Greek view of the hereafter in the pre-Christian era.

1. The poems ascribed to Homer (eighth century BC)

   In the *Iliad* and the *Odyssey* the term *psychē* ("soul") describes a person at and after death, when the soul is snatched away to the unseen world (Hades) as an "idol," a shadowy "double" that lacks the consciousness and mental activity that marked life on earth. Only a person's reputation survives their physical life. The punishment of Tartarus is reserved for those guilty of serious offenses, while the Islands of the Blest belong to divine heroes.

2. The Orphic religion

   When worshipers in the Orphic religious brotherhoods of Greece became totally absorbed in the wild dances and processions of what was known as Dionysiac rites, they sensed they were "standing outside themselves," the literal meaning of the Greek term *ekstasis* (that gives us the word *ecstasy*). To be immersed in such ecstatic worship was to be free from the limitations of time and space, as well as from embodiment. In the hereafter, freed from embodiment, the soul would participate in eternal communion with the particular god whose rites had been followed on earth. The soul was thought to be essentially divine, exiled by embodiment from the societal bliss of souls in heaven. This view is encapsulated in the famous Orphic pun *sōma sēma*, "the body is the tomb (of the soul)" (Plato, *Cratylus* 400C).

3. Plato (d. 347 BC)

   In Plato's view the soul is tripartite, having three forms or functions:

   a. the rational "part" (= reason), that is preexistent, immortal, incorporeal, and self-conscious. It occupies the invisible realm of the divine, and so is prior to the body that has relations only to the visible and physical world that is doomed to perish. The individual person can lay claim to being immortal as a result of having a rational soul but only death releases them from corporeality. For more detail and for references to Plato's works, see below IV.I.

b. the spirited/courageous function; and

c. the appetitive (= desires and affections) function.

These three functions Plato compared to a charioteer (reason) with two unequally yoked horses, one good (courage), and one bad (physical desires) (*Phaedr* 246A–D). If the body has polluted the rational part of the soul by its sensual pleasures, the soul must do penance by successive rebirths until its purification (*katharsis*) when it "regains its wings" and returns to the invisible realm of Ideas or Forms in the ever-present now. Although Plato can juxtapose the concepts of the immortality and the reincarnation of the individual soul, there is no place for the concept of the resurrection of dead persons.

For a comparison of Plato's and Paul's views on immortality, see below IV.I.

4. Aristotle (d. 323 BC)

According to Aristotle, all living organisms—plants, animals, and humans—share the "principle of life" (*psychē*, "soul") and experience growth and decay by being dependent on nourishment. Plants have the nutritive or vegetative soul, while animals have the sensitive or appetitive soul that produces sensation and desire, in addition to having the nutritive soul. But only humans have the rational soul that enables thought and intellect (*nous*), as well as having the appetitive and nutritive soul. Memory belongs wholly to the "passive intellect" (*De Anima* 408B) so the disembodied and immortal "active intellect" (*De Anima* 415A) has no self-awareness and no link with the former bodily existence. Only impersonal reason or the divine *nous* survives the individual's death.

From the evidence of epitaphs it seems most Greeks were uninfluenced by the complex philosophical ideas of Plato or Aristotle but rather shared vague Homeric ideas of the afterlife. Heroes and infamous wrongdoers might have special destinies suited to their deeds, but people in general survived death as bodiless and shadowy "doubles" in Hades, without personal consciousness or identity.

5. Two Greek reactions to "resurrection" (Acts 17:22–34)

In his record of Paul's speech before the council of the Areopagus in Athens, Luke records two dramatically different reactions of the councillors to Paul's mention of "the resurrection of the dead" (*anastasis nekrōn*): "Some of them began jeering, but others said, 'We want to hear you again on this topic'" (Acts 17:32). The "some" who reacted in outright mockery may have been followers of Epicurus (341–270 BC) (Acts 17:18) who believed natural phenomena could all be explained by natural causes so that a personal deity who intervened in the physical world by raising the dead was an absurdity: soul and body simply disintegrated into their constituent atoms at the moment of death. For Epicureans, "the resurrection of the dead" would have meant "the reanimation of corpses"; Paul was dismissed as an "intellectual scavenger" (*spermologos*, Acts 17:18a).

But the "others" who reacted in cautious curiosity were probably Stoics who assumed Paul was "a herald of foreign deities" (Acts 17:18b). They believed that the supreme and impersonal Deity or world-principle that animates all things was known by many names as local and national gods, and that moral virtue consisted in living in accordance with nature and reason. Stoicism lacked any formal doctrine of immortality, but the soul was thought to survive the death of the body. Because Paul had preached "the good news about Jesus and his resurrection," his hearers assumed he was introducing two new deities at Athens: "the Healer" (*'Iēsō*, the Ionic form of the name of the goddess of health and healing, *'Iasō*) and his consort "Restoration" (*Anastasis*) (Bruce, *Acts* 331 and n. 35).

The dominant Greek attitude to resurrection is aptly summed up in the observation of the god Apollo at the founding of the court of the Areopagus in Athens: "Once a man is slain by death and the dust has drunk up his blood, there is no coming back to life" (*anastasis*) (Aeschylus, *Eumenides*, lines 647–48).

C. Roman Concepts

One distinctive characteristic of Roman religious views was an openness to foreign influences, a propensity to assimilate ideas from the peoples they conquered, particularly the Greeks. Like the prevailing popular Greek view, the Roman masses seem to have believed that the soul, rather than being destroyed along with the body at death, survived in an underworld kingdom of the ancestral spirits of the dead (in the case of the Romans, the *Di Manes*, "the divine spirits of the departed"). For the Roman citizen on the street, the hereafter was a cheerless realm whose inhabitants lacked individual distinctiveness and so suffered no judgment and gained no reward. If any gods existed, they were uninterested in human conduct and destiny.

But whatever the status of the deceased person, whether slave or senator, the Romans regarded the meticulous performance of funeral rites as mandatory. This strong sense of obligation was prompted by a desire not only to honor the dead but also to avoid the fearful machinations of the *lemures*, the malevolent and wandering spirits of the dead.

As a result of successive defeats in warfare in the third and second centuries BC, such as the Second Carthaginian War, any belief in the protective intervention of the gods or even the existence of the gods was progressively diminished, although official worship of the gods continued and outward ceremonies were maintained. By the end of the Republic, many Roman writers denied the existence of the gods along with any personal life after death. Catullus, for instance, says that after death there is merely "the sleep of unbroken night" (5.6) and Sallust affirms that "neither anxiety nor joy has a place beyond the grave" (*Bellum Catilinae* 51.20). The poet Vergil is an exception, for in book VI of the *Aeneid* that is partially dependent on book XI of Homer's *Odyssey*, Vergil describes the various regions of the Lower World, with Tartarus depicted as a place of torment for the wicked and for those who repudiated the gods, and Elysium described as a realm of endless delights for the virtuous and the bravest of heroes, while the majority found themselves in the Asphodel Fields that were neither pleasant nor unpleasant.

Later, in the first century of the Empire, in spite of Augustus's revival of religion, the same earlier negative sentiments about the hereafter dominated popular thought. Agnosticism or at least ambivalence about any afterlife was the dominant outlook. In funerary inscriptions of the Imperial Age we can discern the influence of Epicurean thought: death simply ends suffering and misfortune. Conventional nihilistic inscriptions often read "NF NS NC," an abbreviation of the Latin *non fui, non sum, non curo*, "I had no existence, I do not (now) exist, I do not care." A similar sentiment is expressed by Pliny the Elder, who declares that "neither body nor mind has any feeling after death" (*Historia Naturalis* 7.54.188–89) (specific references are from W. W. Hyde, "Roman Ideas of the Hereafter," *The Classical Weekly* XXXIX 20 [1946], 160).

D. *Jewish Concepts*

If the reader wants more detail regarding the OT and intertestamental concepts of death and the afterlife than is summarized below, they are encouraged to consult Harris, *Resurrection*, 45–79 (and the detailed footnotes).

1. Old Testament

Unless a person dies prematurely or violently, death is regarded as normal (2 Sam 14:14), yet as the penalty for sin (Gen 2:17; 3:3) it is unnatural. At death everyone "goes down" to Sheol, the subterranean realm of departed spirits. Death destroys all meaningful existence but not existence as such. Some scholars believe Sheol was compartmentalized, so that it is called "the pit" and a place of darkness and silence when it depicts the permanent abode of the ungodly (Num 16:30), whereas it means "the grave" in connection with the death of the righteous (Gen 37:35).

There is no distinct word for "immortality" in the OT but a coined word is found in Prov 12:28—"not-death" (*'al-māwet*): "On the road of righteousness is life; and the treading of her path is (or, brings) immortality." Here, as elsewhere (e.g., Ezek 18:9, 19, 21), "life" or "live" may refer to prolonged earthly life (as in Deut 6:2; 11:9) or the permanence of one's name or one's progeny. But when the psalmist speaks of "life forevermore" (Ps 133:3) or "eternal pleasures" at God's right hand (Ps 16:11), the immortality of the individual must be in view.

In relating resurrection to immortality, Dan 12:2–3 is distinctive in the OT.

> [2]And multitudes—those who (explicative *min*) sleep in the dusty earth—will awake: some to everlasting life, some to shame and everlasting contempt. (cf. John 5:28–29)

> [3]Those who are wise will shine like the brightness of the heavens, and those who lead many to righteousness, like the stars for ever and ever. (cf. Matt 13:43)

The bodily transformation of the righteous and their resulting indestructibility are implied, as is the mere reanimation of the unrighteous.

With regard to "resurrection" in the OT, on three occasions a miraculous reanimation is recorded (1 Kgs 17:17–24; 2 Kgs 4:18–37; 13:20–21), presumably followed by renewed physical life on earth until death occurred a second time; two righteous people are transported from earth to heaven without experiencing death (Enoch, Gen 5:24; Elijah, 2 Kgs 2:10–11); while the conjuring up of the spirit of Samuel by a medium at Endor (1 Sam 28:3–25) provides evidence of Israelite belief in the survival of individuals beyond death—Samuel appeared "as an old man wearing a robe" (1 Sam 28:14). In eight passages there are clear indications of belief in the resurrection of dead persons (Job 19:26; Pss 17:15; 49:15; 73:24; Isa 26:19; 53:10–12; Dan 12:2; 12:13) (on these verses, see Harris, *Resurrection*, 52, 55–59, 64, 66–68). Sometimes it is merely a case of revivification of a corpse, but at other times transformation after revivification/reanimation. Only once is a general resurrection in view (Dan 12:2). But never does the concept of resurrection occupy a central place in the OT, as it does in the NT, especially in relation to Jesus Christ.

2. Intertestamental concepts

This period (roughly between 200 BC and AD 100) represents an advance on OT concepts and forms a bridge between the OT and the NT with regard to views of the afterlife. Customarily a distinction is drawn between the views of Palestinian Judaism and Diaspora (or Hellenistic or Alexandrian) Judaism, but there was variety within each branch and substantial similarity between the two branches. It was not simply a case of resurrection of the dead (Palestinian) as opposed to the immortality of the soul (Diaspora). (The following threefold classification is from part 1 of H. C. C. Cavallin, *Life after Death: Paul's Argument for the Resurrection of the Dead in 1 Corinthians 15* [Lund: Gleerup, 1974].)

a. Some texts emphasize or refer exclusively to immortality: Palestinian Judaism (e.g., Jubilees and the Testament of Moses); Diaspora Judaism (e.g., 4 Maccabees and Wisdom of Solomon).

b. Texts where the ideas of immortality and resurrection are juxtaposed without any effort to harmonize the concepts: Palestinian Judaism (e.g., Testaments of the Twelve Patriarchs and 1 Enoch 91–104); Diaspora Judaism (Testament of Job).

c. Texts where the ideas of immortality and resurrection are explicitly interrelated: Palestinian Judaism (e.g., Psalms of Solomon and Apocalypse of Ezra); Diaspora Judaism (e.g., 2 Maccabees and Slavonic Enoch).

But other intertestamental writings lack any reference to resurrection when it would be appropriate or expected (e.g., from Palestinian Judaism, Tobit and 1 Maccabees; and from Diaspora Judaism, 1 Esdras in LXX and the Letter of Aristeas). Some texts reproduce the traditional doctrine of Sheol where all souls remain forever as spirits without bodies or spirits with shadowy bodies (e.g., from Palestinian Judaism, Ecclesiasticus; and from Diaspora Judaism, 1 Baruch). But most Jewish texts of this period depict a future resurrection, stressing either the identity between the body buried and the body raised or the glorious transformation of a resuscitated body, involving the righteous within Israel or all Israelites or even all humans. Any resurrection enabled people to appear before God and receive suitable rewards or punishment.

II. Death

A. Terminology

The basic NT terms denoting literal or metaphorical death are *thanatos* ("death") and *apothnēskō* ("die," "face death"). But other words refer euphemistically to death as departure (*exodos*, Luke 9:31; 2 Pet 1:15) from earthly embodiment or from among the living. Sometimes this departure is expressed by a tenting metaphor: "For we know that when our tent dwelling is dismantled (*katalythē*) . . ." 2 Cor 5:1); "I know it will soon be time for the discarding (*apothesis*) of my tent" (2 Pet 1:14). Elsewhere, a nautical metaphor seems to be used: "It is my desire to weigh anchor (*eis to analysai*) and be with Christ" (Phil 1:23). Or perhaps even a metaphor drawn from travel or warfare: "The time for me to break camp (*analysis*) is near" (2 Tim 4:6).

To describe death using verbs, the NT occasionally uses the periphrasis "taste (*geuesthai*) death" (e.g., Matt 16:28; Heb 2:9) and "see death" (*idein*, Luke 2:26; Heb 11:5; *theōrein*, John 8:51). The passive form *koimaomai* ("be asleep," "sleep," "be dead") can also mean "fall asleep," "pass away," "die" (John 11:11; 1 Cor 11:30; 1 Thess 4:13). Whereas the NT epistles use the regular form *apethanen* ("he died") in speaking of Christ's death (e.g., 1 Cor 15:3; 1 Thess 4:14), the Evangelists avoid this pedestrian term, apparently wanting to highlight the uniqueness and remarkable nature of Jesus's death experience in that he chose

11

the immediate circumstances and time of his death. So we find the statements that Jesus "expired" (*eksepneusen* in Mark 15:37, 39; Luke 23:46; from *ekpnein*, "breathe out one's life," "breathe one's last [breath]"/"expire"), Jesus "yielded up (*aphēken* from *apheinai*, "give up") his spirit" (Matt 27:50), and Jesus "gave up (*paredōken* from *paradidonai*, "give up," "surrender") his spirit" (John 19:30).

So potent and pervasive is death's influence that it can be depicted as a realm where Satan reigns (Heb 2:14; Rev 20:13) and can be personified as an enemy combatant with a stranglehold on humanity (Acts 2:24; 1 Cor 15:26), as a horse rider with catastrophic power (Rev 6:8), and as a dominant ruler (Rom 5:14, 17).

B. *Four Types of Death*

1. Physical death

On occasion "death" may refer to a process, the gradual weakening of one's physical powers (2 Cor 4:12, 16). But more commonly it denotes an event, the final and irreversible cessation of bodily functions (Luke 7:12, 15; Phil 1:21; 2:27, 30; Heb 9:27, "people are destined to die once"). Death involves the loss of physical corporeality: we are no longer "in the flesh" (*en sarki*, 2 Cor 10:3). It also involves the loss of earthly corporateness: we are no longer "in Adam" (*en tō Adam*, 1 Cor 15:22). Death can be said to "reign" in the human race (Rom 5:14, 17) by means of the devil "who holds the power of death" (Heb 2:14) as "the ruler/prince of this world" (John 12:31; 14:30; 16:11).

From the perspective of the living who saw the dead person buried or cremated, all of the dead are temporary residents in the grave (John 5:28–29; 1 Thess 4:16–7) or in Hades (Acts 2:27, 31), the lower world, the invisible realm in the heart of the earth (Matt 12:40). But from the perspective of a faith that sees the invisible, the dead are immediately in God's presence, be that described as residence in eternal abodes

(Luke 16:9) or in the Father's house (John 14:2) or fellowship with Christ in paradise (Luke 23:43) or heaven (John 12:26; 2 Cor 5:8; Phil 1:23). See further below, pages 23–25.

Self-inflicted physical death (suicide) is not often mentioned in the OT—only Abimelek (by his armor-bearer, Judg 9:54), Saul (by falling on his sword, 1 Sam 31:4), Ahithophel (by hanging, 2 Sam 17:23), and Zimri (by fire, 1 Kgs 16:18). The only NT instance is the case of Judas Iscariot (see Harris, *Texts (2)*, 37–38).

2. Spiritual death

This depicts people's lack of responsiveness to God (Matt 8:22; John 5:24–25; Rom 6:23; Rev 3:1) and their hostility to God as sinners (John 8:21, 24; Rom 5:12; Eph 2:1) who deserve his wrath (Eph 2:4). Death as alienation from God came on the human scene as a result of human sin (1 Cor 15:21).

3. Death to sin

As a result of being alive to God through dying and rising with Christ, believers are to count themselves as "dead to sin," as no longer slaves to sin (Rom 6:4, 6, 11, 13–14). Ideally, all relation to sin has been suspended; they are unresponsive to the appeal and power of sin but alert and responsive to the promptings of the Holy Spirit.

4. The "second death"

This refers to the final state of those who have already experienced physical death and whose state of spiritual deadness was not reversed during their lifetime through repentance and regeneration. Their "eternal destruction" involves being permanently shut out from the presence of the Lord, the only and endless source of pure joy (Matt 10:28; 2 Thess 1:9; Jas 5:20; Rev 2:11; 20:6, 14; 21:8).

C. Jesus's Encounters with Death

1. The Widow of Nain's Son (Luke 7:11-17)

   Accompanied by his disciples and a large crowd, Jesus met a funeral cortège that was emerging from the small village of Nain to bury a young man at a burial site outside the town. Touched by the mother's grief at the premature death of her only child, Jesus halted the procession by actually touching the bier, thereby becoming ritually unclean (cf. Num 19:11, 22). By his spoken word ("Young man, I say to you, get up!" Luke 7:14) Jesus effortlessly reanimated the dead man (contrast 1 Kgs 17:21). There was full restoration to life: "the dead man sat up and began to talk" (Luke 7:15); movement and speech indicate physical and mental alertness. As an account of the instantaneous reanimation of a corpse that caused everyone to be "awe-struck" (Luke 7:15), the narrative is remarkably restrained.

2. The Daughter of Jairus

   All three Synoptic Gospels record the miracle of Jesus's re-vivification of the daughter of Jairus: Matt 9:18-19, 23-26; Mark 5:21-24, 35-43; Luke 8:40-42, 49-56. As we compare the three narratives, the following story emerges.

   > A synagogue president named Jairus approached Jesus as a desperate suppliant with a request that he should come and heal his seriously ill twelve-year-old daughter who was "at death's door." Jesus began to follow him but was delayed by an incident involving a woman suffering from a hemorrhage. On entering the ruler's house and hearing the commotion caused by people weeping and wailing loudly, Jesus rebuked those who were now mourning the young girl's death and declared that she was not dead but asleep. This prompted their mockery. Taking the girl by the hand, Jesus addressed her with the directive, *"Talitha koum"* ("My child, get up!"), and immediately she stood up.

In declaring "she is not dead but asleep," Jesus is indulging in ironic hyperbole, suggesting that in this girl's case death was like sleep in that it was not permanent and would end with an awakening (cf. John 11:11–14). All three Evangelists indicate that the girl was dead (Matt 9:18; Mark 5:35; Luke 8:49, 53), so the miracle is not simply healing from a terminal coma.

3. Lazarus (John 11:1–44)

This record of the raising of Lazarus is the final sign in the first part of the Fourth Gospel that is commonly known as "The Book of Signs" (John 1:19—12:50).

On the fourth day after Lazarus's death, Jesus approaches Bethany and is met by Martha and Mary, who both independently reflect, "Lord, if you had been here, my brother would not have died." A vivid sense of anticipation is created by Martha's confidence that "even now I know that whatever you ask from God, he will give you"; by Jesus's reassurance "I am the resurrection and the life"; and by his question "Where have you laid him?" After ordering the stone to be removed from the tomb, Jesus offers God his thanks and addresses Lazarus with the words "Come out!" Lazarus emerges, bound in graveclothes, and Jesus then directs him to be released.

On the historicity of these three miracles, see Harris, *Resurrection*, 84–85, 87–90; Murray J. Harris, "'The Dead are Restored to Life': Miracles of Revivification in the Gospels," in *Gospel Perspectives: The Miracles of Jesus*. Vol. 6. Eds. David Wenham and Craig Blomberg (Sheffield: JSOT, 1986) 295–326.

All three miracles are reanimations or revivifications, not resurrections in the full NT sense of a return to life that is irreversible, permanent, and transformative. All the three persons involved gained a new lease of physical life, with health and strength restored, but death finally remained their lot; John actually mentions subsequent plans of the chief priests to kill Lazarus (John 12:10). Nevertheless, the episodes illustrate the complete sovereignty of Jesus over physical death as it affects children and adults, male and female, and parent–child and brother–sister relations. This full mastery is demonstrated by his raising one person from a deathbed, another from his funeral bier, and another from the grave. His potent spoken word was the sole means by which the reanimations were performed: "Young man, I say to you, get up!" (Luke 7:14); "Little girl, I say to you, get up!" (Mark 5:41); "Lazarus, come out!" (John 11:43).

In this same category of revivification we should place the reanimation of "many holy people" at the time of the death of Jesus (Matt 27:52–53) (on this episode see Harris, *Texts (2)*, 14–16).

4. Jesus's Experience in the Garden of Gethsemane

After Jesus had delivered his "farewell discourse" (John 13:31—16:33) and prayed for his followers (John 17:6–26), he and his disciples crossed the Kidron Valley and entered the secluded garden that was called "the place of the oil-press" (Gethsemane). It had become a favorite quiet retreat sanctuary for them all (Luke 22:39; John 18:1–2).

Kneeling in prayer as he envisioned his imminent suffering and confrontation with death, Jesus "was seized by utter dismay and deep distress" (*ērxato ekthambeisthai kai adēmonein*, Mark 14:33). To Peter, James, and John he confided, "My soul is overwhelmed with sorrow (*perilypos*) up to the point of death" (*eis thanaton*, Mark 14:34). This latter Greek phrase indicated that Jesus's intense agony of soul brought him to the very threshold of death. His sweat dripped like clotted blood and an angel was despatched from heaven to strengthen him physically (Luke 22:43–44), lest he die in Gethsemane. In Luke 22:44 ("being in anguish") we have the only NT use of the word *agōnia* that refers to mental torment in the face of impending ills. As Jesus contemplated his coming death on a Roman cross, he was not consumed by fear of the coming physical pain, as intense as it would be—like most of his contemporaries he would have witnessed crucifixions at a distance—but he was cringing from the dread of temporary separation from his Father (cf. Matt 27:46) when he became the God-ordained sin-bearer. As the source of pure light (Acts 3:15; Rom 14:9), he was about to be enveloped in the darkness of God-forsakenness. As the source of all life, he was about to "taste death for the benefit of everyone" (Heb 2:9). Nothing could have been more foreign to Jesus than the experience of physical death— especially death as the bearer of God's wrath. Luke 12:50 ("I have a baptism to undergo, and what constraint I am under until it is completed!") indicates the distressing constraint (*pōs synechomai*) Jesus was perpetually under during his life (his "continuous Gethsemane") until its termination in his final "baptism" of suffering in Jerusalem (cf. Mark 10:38).

5. Jesus's Experience at Golgotha

The name of the site where Jesus was executed was Golgotha, from the Aramaic word *gulgoltā* meaning "(Place of the) Skull" (John 19:17); apparently the place resembled a skull. The English word "Calvary" derives from the Latin word *calvaria*, "skull."

On his arrival at Calvary Jesus would have been suffering from extreme exhaustion, nearing the point of total collapse. He had recently survived the wrenching agony of Gethsemane only through angelic intervention (Luke 22:41–44). He had been without food, liquids, and sleep for twelve hours during the relentless mock trials. Exhausted by the traumatic and unrelenting flogging of the Roman soldiers (John 19:1) (a scourging that sometimes led to death), he repeatedly staggered under the weight of the crossbeam (estimated to be between 70 and 120 lbs) until a soldier forced a passerby to carry it (Matt 27:32).

Although the iron spikes that pierced the wrist or forearm and the feet avoided major arteries, the three nail sites became the centers of excruciating pain. As Jesus gasped for air (with his *exhaustion asphyxia*) by raising himself on his impaled feet, the scourging wounds on his back would scrape against the rough upright beam, intensifying the pain. Already the impaled crown of thorns and the soldiers' beating of Jesus about the face and head (Matt 27:29–30) would have triggered the infamous *trigeminal neuralgia*, the most horrendous pain known to humans that involves stabbing pains across the face comparable to electric shocks.

D. *Jesus's Teaching about Death*

On occasion Jesus referred to physical death as "sleep" (John 11:11–13), in that both end all relation to the physical world and issue in an awakening.

Believing in Jesus and living according to his teaching prevents one from experiencing final spiritual death, the "second death" of ultimate separation from God: "Very truly I tell you, whoever obeys my word will never see death" (John 8:51); "Whoever lives by believing in me will never die" (John 11:26). The positive corollary of this is that the person who believes in Jesus will "live (= experience new spiritual life, both now and in the life to come), even though they die" (physically) (John 11:25b). These two realities—"will never die" and "will live"—come about because of the truth of Jesus's claim "I am the resurrection and the life" (John 11:25a). Whoever believes in God and his messenger's tidings "has eternal life and will not be judged but has crossed over from (spiritual) death to (spiritual) life" (John 5:24).

"I solemnly assure you, today you will be with me in paradise" (Luke 23:43). This is the second of the seven statements made by Jesus during his crucifixion. It was Jesus's response to one of the two criminals who were crucified with him, who had made a persistent request (*elegen*) to Jesus, "Remember me when you come into your kingdom" (Luke 23:42). He had acknowledged his own guilt, with repentance implied, and had recognized Jesus's innocence (Luke 23:41) and was now expressing his belief in the kingship and sovereignty of Jesus in the afterlife. Jesus's promise to this repentant criminal is that "today" (the day of their death) he would depart and take up residence with the resurrected Jesus in his kingly paradise. (The order of the Greek words indicates that "today" belongs with the phrase "with me," not with "I solemnly assure you.") "Paradise" here refers to the place where the righteous dead live in the presence of God. It may be the third (= the highest) heaven or a section of the third heaven (see 2 Cor 12:2, 4).

Clearly, then, in the view of Jesus, death involved both a departure and an arrival. A departure implies a destination as well as an evacuation, a "to" as well as a "from." Physical death does not leave the believer homeless but simply brings a magnificent change to the location of their residence. Paul wholeheartedly concurs with Jesus on this basic point (see below, pages 24–25).

Jesus's teaching about death simply confirms what we deduce from his actions—that although physical death wreaks havoc among the human race, it is ultimately subject to the Prince of life whose potent word reverses death and grants life. No human falls outside his supreme transforming power—be they children, young people, or adults (see pages 14–16 above).

E. *Paul's Encounters with Death*

1. His stoning at Lystra (Acts 14:19–20)

   Six months into Paul's first "missionary journey" (Acts 13:1—15:35), Paul and Barnabas arrive in Lystra (the summer of AD 47), having recently escaped a plot on the part of the gentiles and Jews in Iconium to mistreat and stone them (Acts 14:5–6). With the absence of a synagogue in Lystra, they began to preach to open-air crowds (Acts 14:7, 11, 13, 19). Because Paul had healed a lame man, the crowd were eager to offer sacrifices to Barnabas and Paul (Acts 14:8–18). But Jews from Pisidian Antioch and Iconium managed to sway this fickle Lystran crowd into thinking that so far from being gods, Paul and Barnabas were detestable swindlers and that Paul as the "chief speaker" (Acts 14:12) deserved to die. So Paul was stoned and then dragged outside the city, presumed

dead (Acts 14:19). But with the intervention of the local believers (that probably included Eunice and her son Timothy;
cf. Acts 16:1; 1 Cor 4:17; 2 Tim 1:5), he was resuscitated and
then returned to the city (Acts 14:20a).

Paul was able to discern spiritual benefit in this brush
with death. From now on he could affirm, "I bear on my body
the scars (*ta stigmata*, "marks") that show I belong to Jesus"
(Gal 6:17; cf. 2 Cor 11:25; 2 Tim 3:11).

2. His affliction in Asia (2 Cor 1:8-11)

From Paul's own description of the "distressing affliction"
(*thlipsis*) that overtook him in the province of Asia, we can
deduce that this direct confrontation with death was unique
in his experience.

a. Elsewhere Paul could openly say "I face death every
day" (1 Cor 15:31) and "I have been exposed to death
again and again" (2 Cor 11:23), but on this occasion
he acknowledges that he "despaired even of survival.
Indeed, in our heart we felt we had received a death
sentence" (2 Cor 1:8-9). Constant exposure to deadly
circumstances is different from a single actual confrontation with death.

b. Elsewhere he could boldly affirm that "nothing is beyond my power as I rely on the strength of him who
makes me strong" (Phil 4:13), but in this case he acknowledges "we were oppressed beyond measure,
beyond our power to cope" (2 Cor 1:8, where there
is a remarkable repetition of *hyper*, "beyond": *kath'
hyperbolēn hyper dynamin*). A similar contrast occurs
when he declares that sometimes he was "perplexed,
but never despairing" (2 Cor 4:8) but now admits that
he "despaired even of remaining alive" (2 Cor 1:8).

c. But in the midst of this "deadly peril," the "God who
raises the dead" intervened to rescue him by a veri-
table resurrection (2 Cor 1:10a) and Paul believed that

similar rescues would occur provided the Corinthians supported him by prayer (2 Cor 1:10b–11).

d. When Paul begins 2 Corinthians, he departs from his usual custom in his letters of expressing his thanksgiving to God for the spiritual welfare of his addressees and recording his prayer requests for them (e.g., Phil 1:3–11; Col 1:3–14). Instead, in the present case he describes his own situation and welfare and solicits his addressees' prayer for himself! This radical departure from his literary custom indicates how overwhelming and debilitating this confrontation with death must have been.

The outcome? Paul gained a deeper awareness of his utter reliance on God in the wake of his abandoned self-reliance (2 Cor 1:9). On the anvil of his experience there had been forged a new regulative life motto: "Our competency comes from God" (2 Cor 3:5). On the possible identifications of this "affliction in Asia," see Harris, *2 Cor*, 164–82, 851–61, where the view is defended that the most probable identification is that it was the first attack of a recurrent malady that he later describes as his "thorn in the flesh" (2 Cor 12:7–9).

3. The raising of Eutychus at Troas (Acts 20:7–12)

At the end of his seven-day visit to Troas Paul met with the local Christians on Sunday in a crowded third-story room for a fellowship meal and a celebration of the Lord's Supper. Because he intended to leave the next day he prolonged his pastoral sermon until midnight. One of his hearers, a young man named Eutychus who was seated on the ledge of a window, began to doze off (*katapheromenos*), fell into a heavy sleep (*hypnō bathei*), then sagged down in sleep (*katenechtheis apo tou hypnou*) before falling to the courtyard below (Acts 20:9). Paul immediately went down, threw himself on the young man (cf. 1 Kgs 17:21; 2 Kgs 4:34–35) and embraced him, chiding the distressed bystanders "Stop making this hubbub—his life is (now) in him!" Some of the congregation, greatly comforted, took the young man home alive.

By this event Paul would have been reminded of (1) the supernatural power of the risen Jesus; and (2) the dramatic difference between miraculous reanimation that led to continued physical life (Acts 20:10b) and the final resurrection on the last day that led to the eternal life of a spiritual body. A comparable distinction had been apparent in Jesus's raising of Lazarus from the grave (John 11:38–44) that was followed by the Pharisees' plan to kill Lazarus (John 12:10) against the backdrop of Jesus's assurance that "whoever lives by believing in me will not ever die" (John 11:26).

For the compelling reasons for thinking that this episode at Troas is a miraculous reanimation after death and not merely a case of concussion followed by resuscitation, see Harris, *Texts (2)*, 51.

Of Paul's three confrontations with death, the first and third are described by Luke and were relatively brief; the second is recorded by Paul himself and was personal, dramatic, and potentially recurrent; while the third was merely an indirect encounter. Not surprisingly, the second encounter was profoundly influential on Paul's view of death (see below, pages 22–25).

F. *Paul's Teaching about Death*

1. Physical death

Reflecting Paul's traumatic brush with death in Asia (see pages 20–21 above), 2 Cor 5:1–10 is the classic NT passage regarding the Christian view of physical death.

Until this time Paul had apparently assumed that he would be among those Christians still alive when Christ returned (1 Thess 4:15, 17; 1 Cor 15:51) (for a detailed defense of this position, see Harris, *2 Cor*, 178–80). Second Corinthians 4:10–12, 14, 16 shows that Paul is aware that at any time in the near future the "working" (*energeitai*) of death (2 Cor 4:12) could reach its climax in his death. "For we know that if our tent-dwelling is destroyed, we have a building provided by God" (2 Cor 5:1). At the time of writing, a pre-parousia decease seemed to Paul more probable than his survival to the advent, although he always entertained the hope of being alive to greet the Lord on his return (Phil 3:20–21).

In chapter 4 of 2 Corinthians Paul has pointed out that even in the presence of mortality and death, spiritual life is operative, through God's transcendent power (2 Cor 4:7, 10–12, 14, 16; cf. 6:9). This theme of life in the midst of death is continued in 2 Cor 5:1–10 where the apostle specifies *three sources of divine comfort* afforded the believer who faces the possibility of imminent death. Paul's own experience is clearly a paradigm for the Christian's experience, given the reference to embodiment, the spiritual body, inheritance, receipt of the Spirit, faith, and accountability to Christ.

    a. Certainty of the possession of a spiritual body: "we know . . . we have a building provided by God, a permanent heavenly home not built by human hands" (2 Cor 5:1). This fourfold description of the "building" (from God, indestructible, heavenly, spiritual) matches Paul's description of the "spiritual body" in 1 Cor 15:38–54. "We have" (*echomen*) points to a future assured possession, viz. receipt of a resurrection body at the parousia or (some believe) at death. This receipt marks the end of the process of weakness and death already operative in his body (2 Cor 4:16).

    b. The present possession of the Spirit as the pledge of final transformation: ". . . so that what is mortal may be swallowed up by life. Now it is God who has prepared us for this destiny by giving us the Spirit as a downpayment and pledge (*arrhabōn*)" (2 Cor 5:4b–5). Certainly, by the use of this common commercial word Paul was not suggesting the Spirit is merely an inferior part of the Christian's inheritance or is a pledge to be returned (cf. Gen 38:17–20). The believer's daily inward renewal and strengthening, effected by the Spirit (2 Cor 3:18; 4:6; Eph 3:16), is God's guarantee that human mortality will be for ever replaced by resurrection life. "He [God] who raised Christ from the dead will also give life to your mortal bodies because of his Spirit who dwells in you" (Rom 8:11).

   c. Death begins a new experience "in the realm of sight" involving departure to Christ's immediate presence where personal fellowship with him is enjoyed (2 Cor 5:7–8). Paul realized that he was absent from the Lord's immediate presence as long as his present tent-dwelling formed his residence (2 Cor 5:6). So it was his natural preference to leave his earthly home and take up residence (*endēmēsai*) in the Lord's immediate presence. This permanent change of residence takes place *immediately after death*:

   i. Verse 6 states that residence in a physical body is contemporaneous with absence from the Lord, implying that when the former ends, so also does the latter. That is, what is implied in v. 6 is stated positively in v. 8: as soon as departure from mortal corporeality takes place (v. 8a), residence in the Lord's presence begins (v. 8b).

   ii. In v. 7 walking "in the realm of faith" (*dia pisteōs*) and walking "in the realm of sight" (*dia eidous*) are presented as opposites, with no interval occurring between the end of the one and the beginning of the other. To cease walking in the realm of faith was to commence walking in the realm of sight, which v. 8b defines as living in the Lord's presence and Phil 1:23 defines as being with Christ. For Paul, death meant the enrichment, not the negation, of life itself. Death allows "in Christ" corporeality to achieve its goal in "with Christ" fellowship. If death removes the Christian from one form of embodiment, the physical, it augments another, since to the "in Christ" embodiment that remains intact through death is added a personal "with Christ" dimension.

The prepositions in the phrases "with (*pros*) the Lord" (2 Cor 5:8), "with (*syn*) Christ" (Phil 1:23, as well as "with [*meta*] me in paradise" (Luke 23:43; see pages 18–19 above), in themselves signify nothing more than a passive, spatial juxtaposition, as when a chair is said to be "with" a table. But when they are used to define the relationship between two living persons (viz. the deceased believer and the exalted Lord Jesus), they denote an active, mutual fellowship that is qualitatively superior to the relationship experienced earlier, during life on earth. The difference between "the dead (who are still) in Christ" (1 Thess 4:16) and Christians who are still alive at the time of Christ's advent is not in their status ("being in Christ") but in the quality of their fellowship with Christ and the degree of their proximity to Christ ("being with Christ").

2. Spiritual death

Spiritual death is basically total insensitivity to God, the absence of any active relationship to God, together with active opposition to him (Col 1:21). Paul describes the Colossians as being at one time "spiritually dead because of your trespasses and because your fleshly sinful nature (*sarx*) was uncircumcised" (Col 2:13). Like physical death, this spiritual "death" is the "wages" or due reward or consequence of sin (Rom 5:12; 6:23; 8:10). Using one's body as an "instrument of wickedness" is evidence of spiritual deadness (Rom 6:13).

3. Dying to sin

If spiritual death is unresponsiveness to God's kind invitations, dying to sin is unresponsiveness to sin's attractive advances, "dying to what once bound us" (Rom 7:6). Christians must constantly regard themselves as dead with respect to sin but alive with respect to God through their union with Christ Jesus (Rom 6:11). Slavery to sin has been replaced by slavery to obedience and righteousness (Rom 6:16–18).

G. *Peter's Encounter with Death* (Acts 9:36–42)

In Joppa (modern Jaffa) there lived a woman named Tabitha (in Hebrew; Dorcas in Greek, both names mean "gazelle") who was renowned in the town for her Christian charity. When she died, two men were despatched by the local disciples to urge Peter to come the ten miles from Lydda to Joppa. What they expected from Peter's visit is unclear, but they were doubtless hoping for some divine intervention, since they would have known of Peter's earlier acts of healing (Acts 3:1–10; 5:12–16; 9:32–35) and they had not anointed Dorcas's body for burial but had only washed it and placed it in an upstairs room surrounded by her generous gifts of clothing.

On his arrival Peter immediately sent all the mourners out of the room (following Jesus's example, Mark 5:40), knelt in prayer, and then addressed the corpse with the words "Tabitha, get up!" (which was only one letter different from Jesus's Aramaic command to Jairus's daughter, *Talitha koum*, "Little girl, get up!" Mark 5:41). The dead woman sat up and Peter presented her alive to the assembled believers. As news of the miracle spread throughout Joppa, many came to faith.

H. *Peter's Teaching about Death*

Just as Paul speaks of death as both departure and arrival (see above, F.1), Peter does the same, using the *-odos* ("going," "way") root: *exodos*, "departure" and *eisodos*, "entry," "arrival." Peter assures his readers that he would "do his utmost" (*spoudasō*) to ensure that after his departure (*exodos*) his readers would always be able to call to mind his teaching (2 Pet 1:15). He also affirms that if his readers "do their utmost" (*spoudasate*) to confirm their calling and election, they will never stumble and will receive a rich entrance (*eisodos*) into the eternal kingdom of the Lord and Savior, Jesus Christ (2 Pet 1:10–11). Also like Paul, Peter advocates dying to sins and living for righteousness (1 Pet 2:24b; cf. Rom 6:11, 18, 20) as a natural consequence of Christ's bearing of human sin on the cross (1 Pet 2:24a). Moreover, even though Christ suffered physical death, he was revived by the Spirit (1 Pet 3:18).

I. *The Christian's Attitude to Physical Death*

The NT data suggest that believers should adopt an ambivalent attitude to physical death: it should be neither feared nor welcomed.

1. *Death should not be feared*, since:

   a. by Christ's first advent, death was robbed of its power (Rom 6:9–10; 14:9; 2 Tim 1:10; Heb 2:14–15; Rev 1:18).

   b. at Christ's second advent, death as the last enemy to be subdued by the reigning Christ will be finally eradicated (1 Cor 15:23–26, 54–55; Rev 21:4);

   c. death brings enriched fellowship with the exalted Jesus (2 Cor 5:8; Phil 1:23) and is a prelude to the receipt of a spiritual body (2 Cor 5:1).

2. *Death should not be welcomed*, since:

   a. as a biological necessity death is one evidence of God's curse on humanity for their sin (Rom 5:12; 6:23; 1 Cor 15:56; cf. Gen 3:19);

   b. it deprives humans of their earthly corporeality and their earthly corporateness, removing them totally and finally from the attractive and reassuring securities of life on earth.

It is natural for Christians who are approaching death in the midst of unrelenting physical suffering to anticipate eagerly the relief from pain that death brings, yet they are not welcoming death itself but the prospect of a pain-free and exhilarating residence with Christ on the other side of death (see pages 23–25 above).

III. Resurrection·

A. Terminology

There are three NT **nouns** meaning "resurrection."

1. *Anastasis*, forty-two uses, always (apart from Luke 2:34) in reference to resurrection from the dead. The term is often qualified by a word or phrase: (a) "of the dead" (*nekrōn*, e.g., Acts 17:32; or *tōn nekrōn*, e.g., 1 Cor 15:42); (b) "from the dead" (*hē ek nekrōn*, Luke 20:35); (c) "of the just" (Luke 14:14); (d) "of life" (John 5:29); (e) "of the unjust" (Acts 24:15); (f) "of judgment" (John 5:29). The prefix *ana-* may bear a spatial sense ("up"), denoting the "standing up erect" of someone who has been in a prostrate or reclining position, but more probably it is temporal in import ("again"), of a coming to life again after a period of death. In the phrase *ek nekrōn* or *apo (tōn) nekrōn* (e.g., Matt 28:7) the notion is not the emergence of bodies from their tombs (but see John 5:29) but the release of persons from the realm of the dead or from death.

2. *Exanastasis*, only one use in the Greek Bible (Phil 3:11). This may simply be a stylistic variant of *anastasis* or may be

---

* The following summaries largely depend on Harris, *Immortality*, 269–72 (used with permission).

emphasizing the imagery of resurrection as "out from among [*ek-*]" the dead.

3. *Egersis*, one NT use (Matt 27:53).

No fewer than eleven **verbs** refer to resurrection of some type.

1. *Anhistēmi*, "raise up," "rise up," the verbal equivalent of *anastasis*. Non-resurrection meanings predominate (66 out of 107 NT uses; statistics here and below from L. Coenen, "Resurrection," *NIDNTT* 3.276, 280).

2. *Egeirō*, "rouse," "raise up," matching the noun *egersis*, 143 NT uses. Like *anhistēmi*, it may signify the raising of the dead to renewed physical life (Mark 5:41; Luke 7:14) as well as to bodily resurrection life (1 Cor 15:42–44, 52). As with *anhistēmi*, the phrase "from the dead" is sometimes attached to this verb. The passive voice of *egeirō* may bear an intransitive sense, so that *ēgerthē* may, like *anestē*, mean "he rose." This translation of *ēgerthē* (in passages such as Mark 14:28; 16:6; Rom 6:4, 9; 8:34; 2 Cor 5:15) does not jeopardize the frequent NT assertions that the Father raised Jesus (e.g., *egeirō*, Acts 3:15; Rom 10:9; 1 Pet 1:21; *anhistēmi*, Acts 2:24, 32; 13:34).

3. *Exegeirō*, "raise up," found only twice (Rom 9:17; 1 Cor 6:14).

4. *Synegeirō*, "raise with," three uses (Eph 2:6; Col 2:12; 3:1), where the prepositional prefix (*syn*) points to similarity of action and identity of destiny. Christians are raised to new life, just as Christ was.

5. *Zaō*, "live," refers to Christ's resurrection (e.g., Rom 14:9) or his present resurrection life (e.g., 2 Cor 13:4), mere reanimation (e.g., Matt 9:18), the receipt of resurrection life (e.g., John 11:25), and the enjoyment of spiritual renewal (e.g., Rom 6:11).

6. *Anazaō*, "come to life again," used once of spiritual resurrection (Luke 15:24), once of the revival of sin (Rom 7:9).

7. *Syzaō*, "live with," used twice of sharing in Christ's resurrection (Rom 6:8; 2 Tim 2:11).

8. *Zōopoieō*, "give life to," denotes the action of God in raising Christ (1 Pet 3:18) or other dead persons (Rom 4:17), or Christ's work of giving his people new spiritual or bodily life (John 5:21; 1 Cor 15:45).

9. *Syzōopoieō*, "make alive together with," used only in Eph 2:5 and Col 2:13, describing believers' receipt of Christ's resurrection life.

10. *Anagō*, "bring up," used twice of Christ's resurrection (Rom 10:7; Heb 13:20).

11. *Ekporeuomai*, "go/come out," used once of the emergence of the dead from their graves (John 5:29).

For further details about all these uses, see Harris, *Immortality*, 270–71.

B. *Five Types of Resurrection in New Testament Thought*

1. The past bodily "resurrection" (= reanimation) of certain individuals to regained physical life (e.g., Luke 7:14–15; see above II.C).

2. The past bodily resurrection of Christ to immortality (e.g., Rom 6:9: "We know that because Christ was raised from the dead, he will never die again").

3. The past spiritual resurrection of believers with Christ (e.g., Col 2:12, "In baptism you were raised with him"; cf. Rom 6:4, 6, 13, 17).

4. The future bodily resurrection of believers to immortality (e.g., John 5:29a; 1 Cor 15:52).

5. The future personal resurrection of unbelievers to judgment (John 5:29b; Acts 24:15).

C. *Three Distinctive Elements in the Past Resurrection of Christ and the Future Resurrection of Believers*

1. Reanimation: the regaining of physical life lost through death. "Women received back their dead, raised to life again" (Heb 11:35).

2. Transformation: the positive alteration of bodily properties and abilities to suit an entirely new and permanent environment, since "flesh and blood cannot inherit the kingdom of God" (1 Cor 15:50). Paul indicates that all believers "will be changed . . . the dead will be raised imperishable" (1 Cor 15:51–52). The change that results in imperishability or immortality is coincident with resurrection—and, in fact, is part of the resurrection event itself (see below pages 69–71).

3. Exaltation: the elevation of the person raised from the dead to a position of unparalleled honor in the presence of God. Just as the resurrected Jesus was seated at God's right hand (Rom 8:34), so resurrected believers will be co-heirs with Christ, sharing in his glory (Rom 8:17).

These three stages of resurrection in its full theological sense are also applicable to believers' past spiritual resurrection (III.B.3 above). From spiritual death the believer is raised up (Eph 2:1, 6) to transformed new life (Rom 6:4) in the heavenly realm (Eph 2:6).

Resurrection, then, is never a process but rather an event that leads to a state. For example, a perfect passive form of the verb *egeirō* ("raise up"), viz. *egēgertai*, occurs seven times in 1 Cor 15 and literally means "he has been raised." It implies a past event, "he rose" (*ēgerthē*), but highlights the present consequences of that event, and so can be rendered "he is risen." When this verbal form *egēgertai* is used with "on the third day" (1 Cor 15:4), English diction requires "he was raised on the third day," but the full sense is "he rose on the third day (event) and remains alive (state)."

D. *The Resurrection of Jesus*

1. The empty tomb

    Several convincing arguments establish the reality of Jesus's resurrection from his tomb some thirty-six hours after his burial.

    a. There are three or perhaps four *independent* literary testimonies to the emptiness of Jesus's tomb—Mark 16:1-8 (the earliest account), Matt 28:11-15 (a widely circulating story arising from the tomb guards' report to the chief priests), John 20:11-18, and probably Luke 24:1-12. While this is remarkably significant, multiple attestation in itself is no guarantee of truth.

    b. When the earliest Christians persisted in proclaiming in Jerusalem that God had raised and exalted Jesus (Acts 2:24, 32-36; 3:13, 15), the failure of the Jews to respond was significant, for they evidently lacked proof that the tomb was still occupied or could not produce witnesses to account for the disappearance and disposal of Jesus's body. Their only response was to assert that there had been "body snatching" (Matt 28:11-15), a claim that presupposes that the tomb was actually empty.

    c. As first-century AD Jews, the earliest Christians would have assumed that any resurrection shortly after death implied an empty sepulcher. All Jewish contemporaries of Jesus would have known that Lazarus could never be raised from the dead until the stone that lay over his burial cave had been removed (John 11:38-44). Paul, for example, could assert Jesus had been laid in a tomb (Acts 13:29) yet had been raised from the dead by God (Acts 13:30).

    d. Although Jews of ancient times venerated the burial sites of prophets and righteous martyrs (e.g., Matt 23:29; Acts 2:29; 1 Macc 13:25-30), evidence is lacking that the tomb of Jesus was ever venerated—this would have been pointless since he was no longer residing in his tomb.

e. In 1930 Franz Cumont published the text of an inscription from Nazareth in Galilee (see F. F. Bruce, *New Testament History*, Garden City, NY: Doubleday, 1971, 301–3). In the inscription the emperor Claudius (who ruled AD 41–54 and was renowned for his antiquarian interests) departs from Roman legal tradition by issuing a decree that pronounces a death sentence for the crime of tomb spoliation and body snatching in Galilee in particular (or perhaps in Palestine generally). It may have been through his close friendship with Herod Agrippa I (Acts 12:1–5) that Claudius came to associate the rise of seditious religious movements like the sect of the Nazarenes (Acts 24:5) with tomb violation. This Nazareth decree, like Matt 28:11–15, presupposes the empty tomb. Both the adversaries and the associates of Jesus agreed that his tomb was empty.

2. Further arguments for the historicity of the resurrection of Jesus

a. The resurrection narratives in the four Gospels have a self-authenticating character. The records of the projected event are remarkably restrained. There is no description of the resurrection itself, and no testimony from any witnesses of the actual event. If the Gospel records were in fact legendary fabrications, we may fairly assume that at least one of the Gospel writers would have contained a detailed account of the actual resurrection—such as is found many years later in at least three documents (from Harris, *Resurrection*, 148–49; used with permission).

—In the fragmentary Gospel of Peter (mid-second century AD):

They [the soldiers] saw . . . three men come out of the sepulcher with two of them sustaining the other, and a [talking] cross following them. The heads of the two reached to heaven, but the head of the one [Jesus] whom they led by hand over-passed the heavens.

—In the reading of Mark 16:4 found in the Old Latin codex Bobiensis (dating from the fourth or fifth century AD):

Angels descended from the heavens, and as he [Jesus] was rising [reading *surgente eo*] in the glory of the living God, at the same time they ascended with him.

—In the London Text (K2) of the Coptic work, "The Book of the Resurrection of Jesus Christ, by Bartholomew the Apostle" (that may date from the sixth or seventh century AD): Death had a conversation with the corpse of Jesus on the second day (Saturday). When asked "Who are you?" Jesus removed the napkin from his face and laughed at Death who then fled away with his sons. After this had taken place again, Jesus rose in the chariot of the cherubim.

b. Another pointer to the Gospels' "ring of truth" is the prominent place given to women in the resurrection story. The first appearance of Jesus was granted to Mary Magdalene (John 20:11–17) while the first angelic appearance and announcement were given to Mary (the mother of James the younger and Joses) and Salome (Matt 28:1, 5–7), and three women were the first to observe the empty tomb (Mark 16:1–3). The testimony of women was only rarely admissible in Jewish legal proceedings at the time, so we may fairly assume that if the accounts of the resurrection were fabrications, priority would not have been assigned to women but to key figures such as the apostles or Peter in particular.

c. Further evidence of Jesus's resurrection may be found in the multiple and varied recorded appearances of Jesus after his death and burial. He is reported as appearing to individuals (e.g., Mary Magdalene, John 20:1, 14–18; Cephas/Peter, Luke 24:34; 1 Cor 15:5a; James, 1 Cor 15:7a), to small groups ranging in size from two (Luke 24:13–31) to seven (John 21:1–2, 12) to eleven persons (Matt 28:16–17; John 20:26–29; 1 Cor 15:5b, the "Twelve"), and to one larger group of five hundred (1 Cor 15:6a), most of whom were still alive when Paul wrote to the Corinthians in AD 55, some twenty-five years after the alleged resurrection. It was reported that he was seen alive by both men and women (1 Cor 15:6a), just outside his tomb (Matt 28:1, 5–8a), in the city (Mark 16:1–8), in the country (Luke 24:13–31), by a lake (John 21:1–13), on a mountain (Matt 28:16–20), and in a locked room (John 20:19–20). His witnesses claimed that he appeared for brief (John 20:26–29) or longer (Luke 24:15–30) periods, in the morning (Matt 28:1, 9), in the afternoon (Luke 24:13–15, 28–29), in the evening (John 20:19), and overnight (Luke 24:28–29), and that during his appearances he engaged in walking and talking (Luke 24:15–27; John 20:14–17), teaching (Luke 24:25–27, 45–49; Acts 1:3), preparing a meal (John 21:9–13), and eating (Luke 24:41–43)—all evidence of his reality.

d. Some potent cause must be found that adequately explains the radical transformation of Jesus's disciples from being embarrassed and bewildered cowards who fled in panic when Jesus was arrested (Mark 14:50–52) to indomitable witnesses whom the Jewish Sanhedrin could not silence (Acts 4:13–21; 5:17–41). What occurred between these two dramatically different states of mind explains the difference: "He [Jesus] appeared to the Twelve" (1 Cor 15:5b). And at a later time, what explanation better accounts for the complete and sudden

change in Saul of Tarsus from being a callous extermi-
nator of Christians (Acts 9:1–2; 26:11) to being a tire-
less herald (1 Tim 2:7; 2 Tim 1:11) of the messiahship of
Jesus (Acts 17:1–3; 26:22–23), than his own confession:
"He appeared to me also" (1 Cor 15:8)?

e. The very existence and survival of the church confirms
the truth of the persistent and central contention of the
early Christians that Jesus the Nazarene rose from the
dead after his Roman crucifixion and that this truth
generated the new faith (e.g., Acts 2:22–24, 31–32;
3:14–15; 4:10; 17:2–3). The historian must take at face
value any movement's "papers of association" that seek
to explain the rise of the movement. No alternative
explanation for the rise of Christianity with its belief
in Christ's resurrection proves adequate. For the Egyptians, Osiris was "raised" from death by his wife Isis in
a reanimation leading to life among the dead, where
he reigns as a mummified god, so that his "new life"
is merely a replica of earthly life and any ritual identification with him after death cannot be regarded as
resurrection *from* the realm of the dead. Gentile phi-
losophers scorned the idea of resurrection, Roman
thinkers resisted any belief in personal existence beyond the grave, and Jewish thought lacked any concept
of a permanent resurrection from the dead before the
final judgment. In none of these sources do we find a
suitable stimulus for belief in the resurrection. We also
need to recall the initial and understandable disbelief of
some of the early followers of Jesus (Luke 24:11; John
20:24–25); gullible fantasizers would never have been
successful in creating a movement with its cornerstone,
"Jesus Christ, risen from the dead" (2 Tim 2:8). It was
not the church that mothered the resurrection of Jesus;
it was his resurrection that mothered the church.

f. At first, the Jerusalem Christian Jews met daily in the temple courts for worship (Acts 2:46; 5:42) and observed the Sabbath. But given the intense commitment of all Jews to the sanctity of the Sabbath, there must have been some decisive occurrence that prompted these Jewish Christians to change their main day of worship from the Sabbath to Sunday. That decisive occurrence was Jesus's resurrection on "the first day of the week" (*eis mian sabbatōn*, Matt 28:1; cf. Mark 16:2; Luke 24:1; John 20:1), Sunday, that became "the Lord's Day" (Rev 1:10) (see Harris, *Texts* (2), 169–70). So significant was this change that a committed Jewish legalist like Saul of Tarsus (Acts 22:3; 26:5) could boldly associate the weekly Sabbath celebration with annual religious festivals and monthly New Moons as all being merely "a shadow of the things that were to come" (Col 2:16–17).

E. *Various Objections to the Reliability of the Narratives about the Resurrection of Jesus Stated and Answered*

1. *"No event of the past is conclusively verifiable."*

It is true that the historian deals with degrees of probability, not absolute certainties. But provided the historical basis for a past event can be shown to rest on a high degree of probability, we can safely regard that event as factual. Unless this were so, we would be thoroughgoing historical skeptics. The cumulative evidence for the resurrection is so compelling that the conclusion that Jesus did rise from the dead is the most plausible interpretation of all the relevant data.

2. *"A supposed miraculous occurrence such as an individual's permanent resurrection from the dead should be ruled out as impossible on* a priori *grounds."*

True, "dead people do not return to life" is a self-evident fact, so that a resurrection contravenes natural law. But historical data could potentially fly in the face of imagined "laws" of nature. The exceptional should not be automatically dismissed as nonhistorical. Even though human history affords no precedent for a dead person's gaining of immortal life, this does not preclude it happening nor does it preclude there being enough evidence to make it reasonable to believe that it happened, even if this exception does not invalidate the general "rule" that "dead people do not return to life."

3. *"The Gospels that describe the activity of Jesus after his resurrection are theological, not historical, documents."*

It is now recognized that all historical writing involves presuppositions, be they philosophical, ethical, theological, or literary. History as "uninterpreted fact" is impossible. Although the resurrection story was not written to quench the thirst of the impartial historian but to stimulate or strengthen personal faith in Christ, this theological purpose does not in itself invalidate historical reliability. The latter must be examined on its own customary grounds.

4. *"Jesus swooned on the cross, perhaps by a self-induced trance, then revived in the cool atmosphere of his tomb, escaped from the sepulcher, and finally 'appeared' to his disciples who interpreted his temporary 'revival' (anastasis) as an actual resurrection."*

The Roman historian Tacitus, often acclaimed as the most distinguishes historian of Greco-Roman times, briefly notes (in his *Annals* 15.44) that the Christians "got their name from Christ, who had been executed by sentence of the procurator Pontius Pilate in the reign of Tiberius." In addition to this external testimony to the reality of Jesus's death, we have the record in the Gospels of the soldier's upward spear thrust into the pericardial sac (John 19:34), an action designed to ensure that the crucified victim was actually dead and so did not need his legs to be broken to prevent breathing. Then we have Pilate's careful questioning of the centurion who had supervised Jesus's death after the procurator had learned of the relative speed of the death (Mark 15:42–45). And it seems incomprehensible that a recently crucified victim with his deadly wounds and lacerated body from the scourging could have created the impression on his disciples that he had conquered death and was worthy of worship (Matt 28:5–6, 16–20; John 20:19–29) rather than being in desperate need of medical attention.

5. *The body of Jesus was stolen for a variety of reasons, either by his disciples (who may have wanted to vindicate their discipleship) or the Jews (who perhaps wanted to eradicate the new faith) or Joseph of Arimathea (who wanted to protect the sanctity of his family tomb).*

Whatever the supposed motive for this tomb robbery, this explanation of the empty tomb faces insurmountable problems. Even if the disciples were able to distract or overpower the Jewish temple police (Matt 28:4), why would they bother to unwind the strips of linen around the corpse and the cloth around the head and leave them there (John 20:6–7)? And would his immediate disciples have all been willing to propagate and then die for what they knew was a gigantic hoax—the claim that their Master was permanently alive?

If some Jews or Joseph as an influential member of the Sanhedrin (Mark 15:43) stole the body, they would be creating or at least stimulating the very rumor they were keen to crush—that the Nazarene was now alive. To refute this Christian claim, they could produce the body or introduce the people who carried out the theft. But if, as a secret disciple (John 19:38), Joseph moved the body from its temporary grave to a permanent one once the Sabbath was over, we may wonder why he chose to do this perfectly legitimate task in darkness and also why he failed to inform the other disciples.

6. *The women mentioned in the resurrection narrative (Mark 16:1) visited the wrong tomb.*

This explanation ignores the explicit statement that Mary Magdalene and Mary the mother of Joseph/Joses, two of the three women who brought burial spices to the tomb when the Sabbath was over (Mark 16:1), had already seen where Jesus was buried (Mark 15:47). If the women mistook the tomb because they had arrived in semi-darkness, it was also too dark for a gardener (John 20:15) to be working. On the other hand, if there was full daylight, these women would not have mistaken the tomb.

7. *The so-called appearances of the risen Christ were purely psychological phenomena, either subjective or objective visions experienced by some of Jesus's disciples who reported their experience as actual encounters with a person.*

At no time after the crucifixion of Jesus were his disciples in a psychological state conducive to subjective visions. They were thoroughly dispirited (Luke 24:17; John 20:11), with their eager expectation about what the prophet Jesus would accomplish for them completely frustrated (Luke 24:19-21). Even the initial news that Jesus was alive was dismissed as "sheer nonsense" (*lēros*, Luke 24:11). They retreated and met behind locked doors, fearing some repercussion from the local Jews (John 20:19, 26). If the imagined "appearances" were actually hallucinations induced by physical circumstances such as lack of food or sleep, why was there a sudden halt to the visions after forty days (Acts 1:3)? Also, is it likely that there were identical hallucinations experienced by small or larger groups at different times and in various places? What is more, according to the records, Jesus was both seen and heard, yet hallucinations account for only sight.

As for the proposal that God provided objective visions ("telegrams for heaven" as they have been called) in the consciousness of Jesus's disciples that convinced them of his spiritual reality, God can scarcely be acquitted of dishonesty, for what was seen (Jesus in some recognizable form) did not correspond to reality (his body decaying in a Jerusalem grave). And could a telepathically induced "objective vision" represent Jesus as walking, talking, and eating? Moreover, how would one account for the persistent conviction that Jesus was alive when the visions had stopped and the generation contemporaneous with Jesus had passed on?

8. *"The accounts of Jesus's postmortem appearances are too far removed in time from the purported reality to be reliable. The passage of time creates fantasies."*

Most scholars date the earliest written account of the resurrection about AD 65 (the Gospel of Mark), some thirty-five years after the "purported reality." But such written records reflect early oral tradition about the resurrection and the appearances. Even if a writer is not contemporaneous with the events described, their record can be accurate if their sources—oral or written—are reliable and are used responsibly.

These thirty-five or so years are relatively insignificant in comparison with the dates of the records about the Emperor Tiberius, the best-known contemporary of Jesus, who ruled from AD 14 to 37. Interestingly, the least satisfactory source of Tiberius's reign is a contemporary record written about AD 30 by the amateur historian Velleius Paterculus, whereas the most valuable sources date from some eighty to two hundred years later: the *Annals* of Tacitus (about 115), the life of Tiberius by Suetonius (about 120), and the best source, the Roman history of Dio Cassius (about 230).

Nor should we overlook the testimony of the one-time radical skeptic Paul of Tarsus, who refers to several appearances of Jesus in one of his letters that can be dated in AD 55 (1 Cor 15:5–8). He will have heard some of that evidence firsthand, shortly after the alleged resurrection itself.

9. Finally, there is the most commonly expressed objection. *"There are serious discrepancies between the accounts of the resurrection found in the four Gospels. This points to the non-historicity of the resurrection itself."*

Examples often cited include the following:

a. Duration of the appearances: one day in Matthew and Luke; eight days or so in John; forty days in Acts.

b. Location of the appearances: in Matthew, Mark, and John 21 they occur in Galilee; in Luke and John 20, in Jerusalem.

c. Number of the appearances: Matthew lists two, Luke five, and John four, while Mark, in the shorter ending that is probably original, omits them altogether.

d. Persons the women found at the tomb: in Matthew one angel; in Mark a young man; in Luke, two men; in John two angels.

That there are differences between the accounts is incontestable. Some account for the variations by pointing to the fragmentary nature of local traditions or the editorial activity of each Evangelist as he utilized various inherited traditions. But neither explanation rebuts the charge that the differences are in fact irreconcilable discrepancies.

Among some scholars there is a vigorous antipathy to the procedure of harmonization. But it remains a reputable literary tool used by all historians as they seek to reconcile differing versions of past events, whether those events be insignificant or of profound import (as in the present case). Not surprisingly, many efforts have been made to harmonize the seemingly irreconcilable accounts of the resurrection of Jesus (see the present author's effort in Harris, *Immortality*, 69–71; reproduced in Harris, *Questions*, 107–9). True, no two attempts at harmonization will agree at every point, given the complexity of the data, but this does not establish the impropriety of the task or the contradictory nature of the evidence. If anything, the disagreement among the harmonizers points to the paucity of the data and the absence of collusion among the Gospel writers that would have been needed if a lie were to be substantiated.

Nor should we forget that even if discrepancies in circumstantial detail were established, this would not constitute proof that the central fact—that Jesus rose from the dead—was unhistorical. Two examples from ancient history will illustrate the point (from Harris, *Resurrection*, 158–59; used with permission).

i. In describing the route Hannibal followed as he crossed the Alps into Italy during the second Punic war, the Roman historian Livy (in xxi.31–37) and the Greek historian Polybius (in iii.50–56) disagree, with the former suggesting a route over Mont Genèvre and the latter a route over the little St. Bernard. In spite of this secondary irreconcilable difference between these two distinguished historians, no modern writer doubts the central fact—that Hannibal crossed the Alps (with soldiers, horses and over thirty elephants!).

ii. There is clear disagreement among ancient writers who describe the circumstances of the Great Fire of Rome in AD 64, regarding the exact location of Emperor Nero when he played the lyre while Rome burned. Tacitus says he was on the stage of his private theater, Suetonius believes the location was the tower of Maecenas, while Dio Cassius asserts that Nero was on the palace roof. Even with these contradictions, no historian describing Nero's reign disputes the basic fact that the emperor "fiddled" and sang while the city was on fire.

So in spite of the seeming inconsistencies between the four accounts of Jesus's rising from the dead—that can, with difficulty, be harmonized—the central fact remains unscathed: some thirty-six hours after his death and burial, Jesus emerged from his tomb in a transformed bodily state and appeared in a recognizable form to certain of his followers.

F. *The Uniqueness of Christ's Resurrection*

It is, at first, mystifying how Luke, the historian, can record and presumably endorse Paul's unambiguous statement that Jesus the Messiah was "the *first* to rise from the dead" (Acts 26:23) when he himself in the first volume of his history of early Christianity had already recounted two previous resurrections from the dead—the widow of Nain's son (Luke 7:11–17) and the daughter of Jairus (Luke 8:40–42, 49–56).

Paul's own assertion in Rom 6:9 solves the mystery. "We know that because Christ was raised from the dead, he will never die again; death no longer holds sway over him." After the widow's son was given back to his mother (Luke 7:15) he presumably resumed a normal physical life, as did Jairus's twelve-year-old daughter (Luke 8:55b–56a). The same was doubtlessly the case with Eutychus once he had returned home (Acts 20:12) and with Lazarus once his grave clothes had been removed (John 11:44). Although there is no record of the subsequent deaths of these individuals, it is clear that it was their lot, even after their miraculous reanimations, to face death a second time. Indeed, after the local crowds had gathered to catch a glimpse of Jesus and Lazarus and many of them were believing in Jesus, "the chief priests made plans to kill Lazarus" (John 12:9–11).

In stark contrast, Jesus did not recommence his previous life in Galilee and Judea after he rose from his sepulcher. His was a resurrection to immortality (1 Cor 15:52), to renewed life in a "spiritual body" (1 Cor 15:44) permanently free from the ravages of decay and death (Acts 13:34). At his resurrection Jesus gained a "body pulsating with glory" (Phil 3:21) so that he now lives "by the power of an indestructible life" (Heb 7:16). Peter expressed a comparable thought on the day of Pentecost: "God raised Jesus to life by unfastening the cords tied by death, because it was impossible for death to keep its grip on him" (Acts 2:24).

The general concept of the priority or precedence of the risen Jesus finds expression elsewhere in the NT—as when he is called "the First" (Rev 1:17) or Alpha (Rev 22:13) or is described as the pioneer of believers' salvation (Heb 2:10) or as being "before all things" or "prior to all" (Col 1:17). But specific reference to his priority in resurrection is found in three places.

In *Col 1:18* and *Rev 1:5* the resurrected Jesus is called "the firstborn from the dead." The "firstborn" (*prōtotokos*) was either the eldest child in a family or a person of preeminent rank such as the Davidic king (Ps 88:28, LXX = Ps 89:27, EVV). Since "firstborn" is followed by "from among the dead" (Col 1:18) or "from/of the dead" (Rev 1:5), the emphasis is more likely to fall on priority in time than supremacy in rank (at least in the Colossians passage), although primacy in time implies superiority in rank, as Col 1:18c would indicate.

In *1 Cor 15:23* temporal priority in resurrection is explicit: ". . . all will be made alive. But each in turn: Christ, the firstfruits; then, when he comes, those who belong to him." Earlier, Jesus has been described as "the firstfruits of those who have fallen asleep" (1 Cor 15:20). In the OT the firstfruits were the initial portions of the produce of the field and flock, which were offered to God in acknowledgment of his ownership of all and in thanksgiving for his generous provision (cf. Exod 23:16, 19; Lev 23:10; Num 18:8, 12; Neh 10:37). Just as the firstfruits formed the initial part of the coming harvest, so the resurrection of Jesus to endless life sets the prototype or pattern for all "those who belong to Christ" who make up the full harvest. Deceased believers will, like their Lord, be loosed from the grip of death to enjoy resurrection life. Correspondingly, those who are alive at the second advent of Jesus will undergo a resurrection-type transformation that changes their "humble-state bodies" into "bodies pulsating with glory" comparable to Christ's resurrection body (1 Cor 15:51–54; Col 3:20–21).

If, then, the resurrection of Christ and the resurrection of believers are intimately connected, can we say that Christ's resurrection is the *cause* of believers' resurrection? There are three personal causes of the resurrection of believers: God (1 Cor 6:14; 2 Cor 4:14), Christ (Phil 3:20–21), and the Spirit (Rom 8:11), although ostensibly impersonal causes are the power of God (1 Cor 6:14b; Eph 1:19–20) and the glory of the Father (Rom 6:4). We can accommodate all these data by distinguishing God the Father, acting powerfully, as the ultimate cause of resurrection, and Christ and the Spirit as intermediary causes.

G. *The Resurrection of Believers*

1. Its nature

a. *Believers' past spiritual resurrection*

At the core of Paul's concept of being "in Christ" is the reality of believers' participation in the four central experiences of Christ as summarized in the earliest apostolic message (1 Cor 15:3–5). Christ *died*, and those "in Christ" died "with him" (Gal 2:19; Col 2:20) in that "our old self was crucified with him" (Rom 6:6). Christ *was buried*, and they were buried with him (Rom 6:4; Col 2:12) as a prerequisite for resurrection. He *was raised*, and they were raised with him (Eph 2:6; Col 2:12; 3:1) so that "we too may live a new life" (Rom 6:4). He *appeared*, and they will appear with him in glory (Col 3:4; cf. Rom 8:18–19).

When Paul observes that "God raised us [believers] up with him [Christ]" (Eph 2:6; Col 2:12; 3:1), the resurrection of Christ itself is not the main focus but rather the spiritual transformation of believers who share in his triumph over sin and death (Rom 6:18) and over all the powers of evil (Eph 2:1–6; Col 3:5–8). Paul could have said, "Since Christ was [once] raised, you too are constantly to rise in newness of life." But as it is, his exhortation to the Colossians is in essence, "Since you were raised with Christ at the time of your baptism, act as resurrected persons by setting your hearts and minds on what belongs to the heavenly realm" (Col 2:12; 3:1–2). Perhaps in the divine estimation believers corporately were raised when Christ the representative human was raised, but that corporate resurrection only becomes a personal reality when the hearts of individual believers are renewed by the Spirit of Christ (Rom 8:9–10). After that renewal of spirit that is grounded in Christ's resurrection, believers should constantly live for the Lord's honor in life or in death (Rom 14:8). But both the resurrection of Christ and the spiritual resurrection of believers "with Christ" are always in the past tense.

b. Believers' future bodily resurrection

i. Its nature

First Corinthians 15 has two clearly defined parts: vv. 1–34 deal with the "that" of the resurrection (*hoti*, "that," found in vv. 4, 12, and 15), and vv. 35–58 treat the "how" of the resurrection (*pōs*, "how," v. 35). Paul begins by stating the premise he shares with his opponents: the resurrection of Christ (vv. 1–11). Then he draws a conclusion from this premise: that the dead in Christ will rise (vv. 12–32), before issuing a warning (vv. 33–34). The second part of the chapter (vv. 35–58) addresses two difficulties with this conclusion: first, the nature of the resurrection body (vv. 35–50); second, the destiny of Christians who are alive when Christ returns (vv. 51–57), before Paul gives a final exhortation (v. 58).

Here and in 2 Cor 5:1–2 the apostle identifies six characteristics of the resurrection body.

(1) Provided by God

Although "God gives it a body" (1 Cor 15:38) refers primarily to the bare seed that is planted in the ground (v. 37), it also applies to humans who, in a sense, are sown in the ground at death. To germinate the seed or to resurrect the body requires divine intervention. The different types of "bodies" in the universe (vv. 39–41) illustrate God's ability to provide humans with bodies different from their earthly bodies. God is the architect and builder of the believer's eternal house (2 Cor 5:1).

This truth is expressed negatively when the resurrection body is depicted as a house "not built by human hands" (*acheiropoiētos*) (2 Cor 5:1), a supernatural structure erected purely by divine agency and belonging to the new creation (cf. Heb 9:11).

(2) Heavenly

The first man, Adam, was earthly in origin (1 Cor 15:48a, 49a) as a living being (v. 45a), made of the dust of the earth (v. 47a), so his descendants are earthlings (vv. 48a, 49a) who bear his image (v. 49a). On the other hand, the second man, Christ, has a heavenly origin (v. 47b) as a life-giving spirit (v. 45b), with his descendants destined to bear his heavenly image (v. 49b). The believer's eternal dwelling comes "from heaven" and will be inhabited "in heaven" (2 Cor 5:1–2). That is, heaven is the natural and normal habitat of the resurrection body. This "heaven" is not simply a condition; it is also, although secondarily, a place. The idea of a resurrected body and the concept of a non-spatial heaven are incompatible.

(3) Spiritual

When Paul describes future heavenly embodiment as being a "spiritual body" (1 Cor 15:44), the crucial issue is the meaning of the adjective "spiritual" (*pneumatikos*). This term is not material in sense, i.e., "composed of spirit," where "spirit" is some ethereal heavenly material. Rather, it bears an ethical meaning, since Greek adjectives ending in -*ikos* have a functional or ethical sense—thus, "empowered and guided by the spirit." Here, "spirit" may refer to the Spirit of God or to the human spirit revitalized by the divine Spirit.

Paul indulges in three potent antitheses in 1 Cor 15:42–43.

The body that is sown	The body that is raised
perishable	imperishable (v. 42)
dishonorable	glorious (v. 43a)
weak	powerful (v. 43b)

(4) Imperishable

The spiritual body, unlike the earthly body, will no longer be characterized by the physical frailty, susceptibility to disease, and irreversible decay that finally issues in death. It will be eternally durable, totally unaffected by the ravages of time, and incapable of deterioration and dissolution.

(5) Glorious

The spiritual body, unlike the earthly body, will no longer be characterized by the embarrassing indignities that are inevitably part of the human constitution, what Paul elsewhere calls the lowly human state (Phil 3:21). Its constitution and functionality will be dignified and spiritual. It will be "glorious," beautiful, and attractive to see, pulsating with heavenly glory because it bears the image of the risen Christ.

(6) Powerful

The spiritual body, unlike the earthly body, will no longer be characterized by physical weakness, frustrating infirmity, and inaccessible goals. Instead, energized by the Spirit, it will enjoy limitless vigor and inexhaustible spiritual power.

To these six characteristics identified by Paul, two may be added.

(7) Angel-like

As Jesus disputed with the Sadducees about the resurrection, he declared that in the life to come men will not marry and women will not be given in marriage; everyone will be "as angels in heaven" (Matt 22:30; Mark 12:25). Not only will there be no new marriages in heaven, apparently, in its resurrected state the body will be without sexual passions and procreative powers ("as angels"). The resurrected righteous will not be sexless, since the preservation of personality, essential in resurrection, requires the retention of sexual identity. Rather, they will be deathless, as the Lukan parallel (20:36) makes clear: "they are no longer able to die, for (*gar*) they are like the angels and are God's children, being children of the resurrection."

(8) Adaptable

The isolated appearances of Jesus to various persons over a forty-day period suggests that the spiritual body, though not normally visible to human eyes, has the ability at will to become visible and tangible to humans, wherever they be. "After his suffering, Jesus presented himself alive . . ." (Acts 1:3a); "Jesus revealed himself" (John 21:1); "He [Jesus] appeared" (Acts 1:3b and nine other NT uses). We find the opposite in Luke 24:31: "Then their eyes were opened and they recognized him. And he became invisible (*aphantos egeneto*) to them" = "he disappeared from their sight" (NIV). See further on this topic, Harris, *Resurrection*, 139–46; *Texts (1)*, 49–51.

To summarize: For believers, God has designed a heavenly spiritual body that will have permanent freedom from debilitating decay, superlative beauty and attractiveness, endless energy and power, and will be deathless and perfectly adaptable to circumstance. These characteristics of the resurrection body, considered together, suggest that all the inhabitants of heaven will be in their prime, whatever their age or physical condition at death, and so will be fully equipped to offer superlative worship and service to God and the Lamb (Rev 5:13; 22:3–4).

This future "body" cannot be simply a physical or fleshly body with five senses and the basic vital organs, a body that is now perfectly controlled by the Spirit, for in that case Jesus would have had a spiritual body before his resurrection. It is better to maintain that the link between the natural/physical body and the spiritual body (1 Cor 15:44) is that the same identifiable person or "self" finds expression in two radically different forms of embodiment. There are two places of residence but only one occupant. Here the "body" is an organ for self-expression that is perfectly suited to the atmosphere of heaven. Personal individuality is preserved, just as personal identity is currently retained during the constant change in the molecular composition of our bodies. "God will raise *us* up" (1 Cor 6:14), "us" as we are at the time of the resurrection transformation. The subject of the successive forms of corporeality is one and the same "self." Those who are destined to bear the image of the heavenly man will not be personally different from those who bore the image of the earthly man (1 Cor 15:49). On this issue of the preservation of personal identity in the resurrection, see further Harris, *Resurrection*, 198–201.

In describing the relation between the physical body and the spiritual body, Paul not only uses the replacement or exchange motif (as discussed above) with the emphasis on *discontinuity*. The physical body may also be said to be transformed into the spiritual body. This metamorphosis motif focuses on the idea of *continuity*: "This perishable body must put on imperishability, and this mortal body must put on immortality" (1 Cor 15:53; similarly 15:54).

The complementary nature of these two ideas—exchange and change—is most clearly displayed in 2 Cor 5.

Exchange /Replacement

"If our earthly tent is destroyed, we have a building from God" (v. 1). "As long as we are at home in the body, we are away from the Lord" (and ultimately our heavenly home) (v. 6). "We would prefer to depart from the body and take up residence with the Lord" (and ultimately in our heavenly body) (v. 8). "So we make it our goal to please him, whether we are at home in the body or away from it" (v. 9).

Change/Transformation

"In this tent we sigh, because we yearn to put on as an over-garment that heavenly dwelling of ours" (v. 2). "Assuming, that is, that when we have put it on, we shall not find ourselves disembodied" (v. 3). "For indeed, as tent-dwellers, we sigh with a sense of oppression because, not wishing to become disembodied, we desire to put on our heavenly dwelling as an overgarment" (v. 4).

ii. The time of its occurrence

(1) At the second advent/parousia

Both 1 Thess 4:15–16 and 1 Cor 15:22–23, 52 identify the time of believers' resurrection as the second coming of the Lord Jesus at the last trumpet call.

(2) At the moment of death

When Paul says "If our earthly tent is destroyed, we have a building from God" (2 Cor 5:1), it is natural to assume that "we have" (*echomen*, present tense) means "we have (at that point)" in the sense "we immediately acquire." Clearly, "we have" cannot refer to a present possession, because it indicates what would become true "if," and only if, Paul's earthly tent was destroyed. With a future acquisition of the resurrection body *at death*, there is no interval of homelessness, just as taking up residence with the Lord (v. 8) follows immediately after departure from the earthly body (v. 8). On this understanding, the second advent or parousia marks the open display of the glorious state of God's children (Rom 8:19; Col 3:4), while the future resurrection involves the assembling together of dead and living Christians in their corporate consummation as the glorified body of Christ.

Confronted with Paul's earlier placement of the resurrection at the second coming of Christ (see (1) above), proponents of this view sometimes argue that the deceased believer, no longer within time and space as we know these realities, will not be aware of any interval between their death and the second advent, so that in their experience "we have a building from God" expresses a reality that transpires immediately after death. Another explanation is that 2 Cor 5, written from the viewpoint of the individual believer, anticipates transformation at death, whereas 1 Cor 15, expressing corporate hope, locates the resurrection at the second advent.

What "part" of a believer survives death and experiences resurrection? That is, what entity represents continuity between the physical body and the spiritual body? Even when the NT speaks of departed believers as spirits (Acts 7:59; 1 Cor 5:5; Heb 12:23) or as souls (Rev 6:9; 20:4), it is not identifying one "part" of a person that survives death, but is referring to the whole person who now, without a physical body, belongs exclusively to the spiritual realm. On this holistic view of the human personality as a psychosomatic unity, individuals do not *have* souls and bodies; they *are* souls and bodies. Death severs the soul/spirit-body unity (cf. Heb 12:23; Rev 6:9–11), until the resurrection reunites the soul/spirit with the new body that is perfectly adapted to its heavenly environment. Some identify this continuity between "now" and "then" as the "inward man" (or "inner nature," RSV, NRSV) (2 Cor 4:16) or as an "ego" that is in relationship with Christ or as the "self" (see above, pages 51–52).

iii. The "intermediate state"

What does the NT teach about the locality and state of believers in the interval (from an earthly viewpoint) between their death and their resurrection at Christ's second coming? Traditionally this interval is called the "intermediate state," although the expression is nowhere found in Scripture. Lying between two fixed points (death and resurrection) and being temporary in duration, it is suitably called "intermediate."

As for *locality*, believers at death are safe in God's hands, expressed as residence "with" Christ (Luke 23:43; 2 Cor 5:8; Phil 1:23). Although this "with-ness" is expressed in these passages by three different Greek prepositions (respectively, *meta*, *pros*, and *syn*), the meaning is the same in each case: active inter-personal communion is implied (see above, page 25).

The bodiless *state* of believers as they await their resurrection bodies is a conscious one. Jesus's story about the rich man and Lazarus (Luke 16:19–31) is set in a postmortem and pre-judgment or pre-resurrection state. Lazarus is comforted at Abraham's side (vv. 22–23, 25), but the rich man is tormented in Hades (v. 23). In this intermediate state, there is, apparently, awareness of circumstance (vv. 23–25, 28), memory of the past (vv. 25, 27–28), and rational thought (v. 30; cf. Rev 6:9–11).

One certainly cannot deduce from the verb "fall asleep" that the interim state is one of suspended animation or loss of consciousness. Sometimes this verb *koimaomai* can refer to physical sleep, "be asleep" (e.g., Matt 28:13). But when Paul is speaking of death, the verb has a "point" or punctiliar sense, "fall asleep" (e.g., 1 Cor 7:39; 15:6, 18, 20, 51), even when the present tense is used: "a considerable number have fallen asleep," or "not a few are, from time to time, falling asleep" (1 Cor 11:30). Believers who die "fall asleep" in that they are no longer active in or conscious of the earthly world of time and space but they are fully aware of their new environment, for they take pleasure in resting from their earthly labors (Heb 4:10; Rev 14:13) and in being "alive to God" (Luke 20:38) and "living spiritually, as God does" (1 Pet 4:6).

In any case, if the "intermediate state" were a period of unconsciousness, we would be unable to explain Paul's preference (2 Cor 5:8) or desire (Phil 1:23) to depart to Christ's presence. Even in the midst of all his sufferings, communion with Christ and active service for him on earth would have seemed preferable to a postmortem state of unconsciousness and inactivity.

Whatever one's view of the "intermediate state," the focus of the NT is on the ultimate, not the penultimate, stage of the divine plan (1 Cor 15:24–28) and on the need for faithful stewardship and readiness for the Son of Man's arrival (Matt 24:42–47).

H. *Unbelievers' Future Resurrection*

1. Its nature

In two places in the NT reference is made to the resurrection of unbelievers. Jesus refers to a coming time when "all who are in their graves" will come out—"those who have done good, to the resurrection (*anastasis*) of life, and those who have done evil, to the resurrection (*anastasis*) of condemnation" (John 5:28–29). In Paul's defense before Antonius Felix (Acts 24:1–27) he declares that he shares the traditional Jewish hope in God "that there will be a resurrection (*anastasis*) of both the righteous and the wicked" (Acts 24:15). In reference to "the wicked," the term "resurrection" clearly cannot signify a rising from the dead that involves sharing eternal life in God's holy presence, for the wicked, such as "anyone who does what is shameful or deceitful," has no place in the Holy City (Rev 21:2, 27). What is signified is a simple renewal of personal life, a "coming to life again" (Rev 20:5), a reanimation or a revivification that enables personal accountability for life on earth (cf. Dan 12:2; Matt 25:46; Rev 20:11–15). All that we can say with confidence is that there will be a resuscitation of "those who have done what is evil" (John 5:29) to enable their appearance before God in some undisclosed form that permits continuity of personal identity. It is clear that the term *anastasis* may on occasion denote a simple restoration to life: "Women had their dead restored to them by resurrection (*anastasis*)" (Heb 11:35). These women of faith probably include the widow of Zarephath (1 Kgs 17:17–24) and the Shunammite woman (2 Kgs 4:17–36).

For the unrighteous, the "intermediate state" is a period of anguish and torment in Hades (Luke 16:23–25, 28) as they await "punishment on the day of judgment" (2 Pet 2:9; cf. John 5:29).

2. Its result

In Scripture "judgment" has two basic senses, one neutral (a judicial evaluation of evidence that leads to either a positive or a negative verdict), and one negative (the examination of evidence that results in a negative verdict and the imposition of a penalty). All people will be judged, both the living and the dead (Acts 10:42; 2 Tim 4:1), on the basis of their relation to Christ (Mark 8:38; John 3:36) and their works during their lifetime (Rom 2:6; 2 Cor 5:10; 1 Pet 1:17). "For those who are self-seeking and reject the truth and follow evil, there will be wrath and anger" (Rom 2:8).

As Paul speaks of the retribution God will exact on the persecutors of the Thessalonian believers (2 Thess 1:6b), he indicates that this divine retribution will occur "when the Lord Jesus is revealed from heaven in flaming fire along with his powerful angels, inflicting vengeance on those who do not know God and on those who do not obey the gospel of our Lord Jesus" (2 Thess 1:7b–8; cf. Heb 10:29) (see further below, page 91).

I. *Traditional Terminology about Resurrection*

1. "Resurrection of the flesh"

   In this expression "flesh" (*sarx*) may denote the fleshly body or the whole person, body and soul, or even all humans. But since in classical Greek "flesh" normally referred to the soft tissue covering of animal or human bones, there is ambiguity in the expression.

2. "Resurrection of the body"

   This traditional formulation perhaps reflects Paul's unique phrase *egeiretai sōma pneumatikon* (1 Cor 15:44) that may be rendered "a spiritual body is raised up" or, better, "it [that is, the body that is sown] is raised a spiritual body" (NASB, NIV). In the latter case, "(resurrection of the) body" will refer to the physical body.

3. "Resurrection of the dead"

   The Constantinopolitan Creed of AD 381, the product of an assembly of over 180 Greek bishops, was admitted as authoritative in both East and West. In this credal statement "the dead" refers to all deceased people, so the allusion is to a "general resurrection." In NT usage this phrase can refer to all the dead (Acts 17:32; 24:21; Heb 6:2) or the righteous alone (e.g., Acts 23:6; 1 Cor 15:42) or even Jesus (Rom 1:4), with the variant construction, "resurrection from the dead (= the realm inhabited by the dead)," found four times, only of believers (Luke 20:35; Acts 4:2; Phil 3:11; 1 Pet 1:3).

   Other formulations have been proposed—such as "resurrection in the body" or "the resurrection of man/the person"—but they are without biblical or credal precedent.

   Of the three major formulations listed above (1, 2, 3), the third is to be preferred, because it has both credal and biblical support (see above); and the qualification "of the dead" is personal in nature and plural in form, hinting at the interpersonal and corporate nature of the resurrection state.

IV. Immortality*

A. *Terminology*

Only three NT terms—two nouns and one adjective—express the idea of immortality.

1. *Athanasia*, by derivation (with the negative prefix a-) "non-dying-ness" or "deathlessness" or "immortality" is used seven times in the LXX (4 Macc 14:5; 16:13; Wis 3:4; 4:1; 8:13, 17; 15:3) but never in the LXX version of the Hebrew canonical Scriptures, since the Hebrew OT lacks any specific equivalent of the word *immortality* (on the coinage *'al-māwet̲*, "not-death," see above, page 8). The three NT uses of *athanasia* are Pauline: God is described as the One "who alone possesses immortality" (1 Tim 6:16), while in 1 Cor 15:53–54 (two uses) believers are depicted as being invested with immortality at the last trumpet. The cognate adjective *athanatos*, "deathless," is found six times in the LXX—again, outside the Hebrew canon (Wis 1:15; Sir 17:30; 51:9; 4 Macc 7:3; 14:6; 18:23)—but does not occur in the NT. Its nearest equivalent is *akatalytos*, "indestructible," found only in Heb 7:16, in reference to the power of Christ's life that was "beyond the reach of death," and in 4 Macc 10:11.

---

* The following summary depends in part on Harris, *Immortality*, 273–75 (used with permission).

59

2. *Aphtharsia*, by derivation (with negative prefix a-, *phthora*, "corruption") "non-decaying-ness" or "incorruptibility" or "imperishability" or "immortality" is found four times in the LXX (Wis 2:23; 6:19; 4 Macc 9:22; 17:12) and seven times in the NT, all in Paul. "Immortality" (*aphtharsia*) describes the divine state (Eph 6:24); it was "brought to light" by Christ as indicated in the gospel (2 Tim 1:10); and it is the gift granted to the righteous (Rom 2:7) when they receive imperishable spiritual bodies (1 Cor 15:42, 50, 53–54).

3. *Aphthartos*, "incorruptible" or "immortal" occurs twice in the LXX (Wis 12:1; 18:4) and seven times in the NT, where it depicts the quality of the divine nature (Rom 1:23; 1 Tim 1:17; 1 Pet 1:23); the gentle and quiet disposition of the Christian woman (1 Pet 3:4); the reward (1 Cor 9:25) or inheritance (1 Pet 1:4) of all Christians; and the future state of resurrected believers (1 Cor 15:52).

B. *Observations about These Terms*

1. All of the ten uses of the two nouns are found in Paul's letters.

2. None of the three terms occurs in the LXX version of the Hebrew canonical Scriptures.

3. Of the seventeen NT uses of these three terms, five apply directly or indirectly to God (Rom 1:23; Eph 6:24; 1 Tim 1:17; 6:16; 1 Pet 1:23), while the other twelve apply directly or indirectly to humans and always (except for 1 Pet 3:4) relate to their future destiny, not their present state.

4. All three Greek terms are formed using the negative prefix *a*—that is comparable in effect to the English *in-* or *un-*.

5. Both nouns denote a quality as well as a state.

—*athanasia*:

the state of being free from the principle of death = deathlessness the quality of being incapable of dying = immortality

—*aphtharsia*:

the state of being free from decay = incorruption

the quality of being incapable of decay = incorruptibility

The person who has *aphtharsia* and *athanasia* is at any given moment free from decay and death and will always remain so. Moreover, the terms are complementary. Those who are immune from debilitating decay will therefore also be immune from death. And those free from the inward working of the death-principle must also be free of its expression in decay.

It is highly improbable that *aphtharsia* ever denotes freedom from *moral* corruption (= *aphthoria* or *adiaphthoria*, purity or integrity of conduct, soundness of doctrine), although Origen and many later Greek commentators understood Eph 6:24 of moral rectitude. In this verse, *en aphtharsia* after "Grace be with all who love our Lord Jesus Christ" probably means "ceaselessly" or "with an undying love" or even "in perpetuity" or "[Christ] who reigns immortal" (in heaven).

C. *The Immortality of God*

Three times the adjective *aphthartos* ("immortal") is applied to God (Rom 1:23; 1 Tim 1:17; 1 Pet 1:23): he is devoid of "corruption" (*phthora*), whether personal or moral; deterioration and death are foreign to his experience. But it is in 1 Tim 6:15–16 that there is an unambiguous assertion of the uniqueness of God's immortality. He is "the blessed and only Sovereign . . . who alone has immortality (*athanasia*)," that is, he has the state of "non-dying-ness" or "deathlessness" and the quality of being incapable of dying. His uniqueness ("alone") as the possessor of immortality means that only by his own gracious initiative in sharing his immortality can anyone else become immortal. He and he alone is the giver of immortality. Any search for immortality apart from God is fruitless.

Behind any explicit negative definition of God's nature lies some implicit positive assertion. Such definition by negation, the *via negationis* ("the way of negation"), has always been recognized as a legitimate procedure. Accordingly, to deny God's mortality by calling him "immortal" is to imply his incessant life. Significantly, the same sentence (in Greek) that ascribes immortality to God (1 Tim 6:16) declares that he "perpetually gives life to everything" (*tou zōogonountos ta panta*, 1 Tim 6:13). Immortality implies the presence of life and energy as well as the absence of death. God is never-dying because God is ever-living as "the fountain of life" (Ps 36:9). "The Father has life in himself" (John 5:26; cf. 6:57) as "the Lord God Almighty, who was, and is, and is to come . . . who lives for ever and ever" (Rev 4:8-9) and as "the living God" who is the creator of the universe and the provider of sustenance for humans (Acts 14:15-17). Inactivity as well as death are absent from God's experience.

A second implication of God's non-mortality is his holiness. Sin and death are natural companions: where there is sin, there is death; "the wages of sin is death" (Rom 6:23). But the reverse is also true: where there is no sin, there is no death. God, being immortal, is untainted by sin. Holiness is a concomitant or corollary of immortality. Immediately after affirming God's sole immortality, Paul continues "[God] lives in unapproachable light" (1 Tim 6:16).

Thirdly, to assert God's immortality is to imply his immutability. If any deterioration of character or deviation of conduct that could lead to death is foreign to God, he is incapable of character change. What he has always been, he will continue to be. But we must remember that although God's intrinsically holy character and righteous conduct cannot change, he can choose to react to change in his created world in a manner consistent with his nature (see Harris, *Texts (2)*, 95-96).

So then, God's immortality implies his ceaseless energy, his inviolable holiness, and his unchanging character.

D. *The Immortality of Humans*

If God alone is immortal by nature (1 Tim 6:16), only by his gift can anyone else become immortal (cf. Rom 2:7; 6:23). So we can affirm that human immortality *in the sense of endless life* is a derived not an essential characteristic.

But did God give humans this gift of the ability to live for ever when he created them? Three different answers have been given, with the third preferred.

1. Humans were created "immortal," but forfeited their immortality when they disobeyed God's directive (Gen 3:1, 6). But it is difficult to conceive of the loss of an "undyingness" already possessed or of the receipt of "permanent immortality" if Adam and Eve had been obedient. Once received, immortality is a permanent and irreversible possession.

2. Humans were created mortal yet were able to become immortal as a reward for obeying God.

3. Humans were created neither immortal (see Gen 3:22) nor mortal (Gen 2:17; 3:3), but could become either, depending on their obedience or disobedience to God. They were created *for* immortality rather than *with* immortality. Adam and Eve disobeyed and so were destined to die physically and spiritually (Gen 2:17; 3:6). Being potentially free of decay and death, humans actually become immortal by God's choice if they are obedient to him. Disobedience robs them of immortality in its full NT sense of freedom from decay and death as a result of sharing the divine life. In the present era, that disobedience is shown by rejection of the truth contained in the gospel (2 Thess 1:8; 1 Tim 2:4; 2 Tim 3:7; 1 Pet 2:8; 4:17). On the other hand, for those who have obeyed "the true message of the gospel" there is the hope (of receiving immortality in its full sense) "that is stored up in heaven" (Col 1:5).

On this third view, humans were not created unable to die (*non posse mori*) but were created able not to die (*posse non mori*), although after the fall they were unable not to die (*non posse non mori*), to use the classical distinctions. Now, after the great reversal effected by Christ, believers will be unable to die since they will be sharing the immortal divine nature (2 Pet 1:4, on which see below, page 66).

All humans are immortal in the sense that they will have a postmortem existence, but only those who have obeyed "the gospel of our Lord Jesus" (2 Thess 1:8) will become immortal in the Pauline sense of having freedom from decay and death as a result of sharing the divine nature. Romans 2:7–8 outlines the two possible outcomes that will follow the divine assessment of works performed (Rom 2:6): "To those who persist in doing good as they strive after glory, honor, and immortality, God will give eternal life. But for self-seeking people who resist the truth and yield to wickedness, there will be wrath and fury."

The implication we may draw from these distinct outcomes is clear. Just as those who pursue immortality will not experience God's wrath, so those who fail to respond to the truth of the gospel will be denied eternal life—which here includes immortality, as the parallelism shows.

These two categories of people with regard to the receipt of immortality are also apparent in 1 Cor 15. The "all" who will be changed by being clothed with immortality (vv. 51, 54) are the dead who will be raised immortal along with those alive at Christ's coming (v. 52). Earlier in the chapter this group has been called "those who have fallen asleep in Christ" (v. 18), "those who belong to Christ" (v. 23), "those who belong to heaven" (v. 48), and those destined to "bear the image of the heavenly man" (v. 49). It is a fair inference that the "some who are ignorant of God" (v. 34) do not belong to Christ and so will not be clothed with immortality. Investiture with immortality is denied to those who are "separate from Christ" (Eph 2:12). It is inconceivable that any who are doomed to undergo the punishment of eternal exclusion from the presence of the Lord (2 Thess 1:9) will simultaneously "participate in the divine nature" (2 Pet 1:4) and so be free of decay and death.

E. *Time of the Receipt of Immortality for Believers*

Three possibilities have been proposed.

1. At regeneration

   The promise of immortality not only came on the scene through the proclamation of the gospel (2 Tim 1:10); it was realized by the individual believer when they were born anew as a result of God's creative sowing of immortal seed (1 Pet 1:23) (reflecting one understanding of this verse). This view can be reconciled with #3 (below) by proposing that the immortality gained *potentially* at the time a person comes to be in Christ (2 Cor 5:17) becomes an *actual* possession at the resurrection of the Christian dead.

2. At death

   Those who maintain that a spiritual body is received by believers at death naturally affirm that immortality is received at the same time.

3. At the resurrection of believers on the last day

   There is more explicit evidence to support this view than either of the foregoing options. First Corinthians 15 juxtaposes resurrection and immortality in fixed order in the phrases "what is raised is immortal" (v. 42) and "the dead will be raised immortal" (v. 52) = "the dead will be raised and [thus] become immortal." If these two statements meant simply "raised as they already are [= immortal]," resurrection would cease to have any significance as a new state.

   An analysis of all six NT passages where resurrection and immortality are explicitly brought together (viz. Luke 20:27–40; John 11:25–26; 1 Cor 15:51–54a; 2 Cor 5:1–4; Heb 11:35; Rev 20:4–6) shows that a resurrection transformation is the only means of acquiring immortality (in the Pauline sense), while immortality is the outcome of every resurrection transformation (for details, see Harris, *Immortality*, 209–32). Immortality is a future divine gift granting freedom from all the decay that leads to death, as a result of participating in God's life. Although the term *immortality* is not used in 2 Pet 1:4, reference is made to its positive and qualitative aspect—unmediated participation in the divine nature. Through the fulfillment of God's "magnificent and precious promises" about the second coming of Christ (2 Pet 1:16; 3:4, 9–10, 12), those who have escaped by death from the world's corruption will become sharers of the divine nature (see Harris, *Texts (1)*, 209).

F. *The Immortality of the Soul*

In spite of the popularity of this concept in Christian thought and its occurrence in some creeds, for several reasons it should not be endorsed as an accurate summary of NT teaching.

1. The three NT terms that express the idea of immortality (*athanasia, aphtharsia, aphthartos*) are never used in conjunction with the word *soul* (*psychē*), as is the word *athanatos* ("immortal") in 4 Macc 14:6; 18:23, but all three are associated with the spiritual body (seven times, in 1 Cor 15:42, 50, 52, 53 [twice], 54 [twice]).

2. In this phrase, "immortality" refers to the survival of the soul beyond death, but in Pauline thought the term *immortality* describes a post-resurrection state of freedom from decay and death as a result of sharing divine life. In one case immortality comes automatically to all people by birth; in the other case, it is God's special gift to the redeemed and results from the "new birth."

3. If immortality is the inherent possession of all humans, it is strange that Paul can affirm that God alone possesses immortality (1 Tim 6:16) and that he grants immortality to certain people as his gift (Rom 2:7; 1 Cor 15:53–54).

4. If the individual human soul is naturally immortal, the corporate dimension of the life to come is easily surrendered.

5. Enjoyment of life after death depends on one's relationship to God (Rom 2:6–7), not on an inalienable human property.

6. If the soul is indestructible, in what sense can God be said to "destroy" the soul in Gehenna (Matt 10:28) or inflict the "second death" (Rev 21:8)?

7. Given the permanent independence of a self-sustaining soul before and after death, various consequences would seem to follow: embodiment becomes unnecessary for survival; dependence on God and accountability to him are removed; death is regarded as emancipation from the restrictions of corporeality; and postmortem existence is simply the continuation of earthly life. All of these concepts are foreign to a Christian perception where believers face divine evaluation before receiving their transformed embodiment for the perfected worship and service of God in a new or renewed heavens and earth (on which see below, pages 87–90, 95–98).

8. A focus on the soul's natural immortality differs radically from Paul's emphasis on the whole person (*sōma*) in their resurrected state as being immortal.

9. No NT writer uses the verb *athanatizō*, "I make immortal" (of God's action) or (in the passive voice) "I am immortal" or "I become immortal" (of the human state). The passive use would have been suitable, for example, in 2 Cor 5:4 (". . . so that what is mortal may become immortal").

G. *Relation of Immortality and Eternal Life*

1. Similarities

Both are God's gifts (1 Cor 15:52; Acts 13:48; Rom 6:23).

Both relate to the heavenly state of blessedness (1 Cor 15:49, 54; Gal 6:8).

Both result from a resurrection transformation that involves the whole person (1 Cor 15:42, 52; Rom 8:11).

Both are received by those who meet certain conditions (1 Cor 15:22–23; Acts 11:18).

2. Differences

"Immortality" is a negative expression, relating to death; "eternal life" is a positive expression, relating to vitality. One term refers primarily to quantity (*a-thanasia*, "undyingness," eternal freedom from death) and secondarily to quality (participation in the divine life). The other refers primarily to quality (*zōē*, transcendent life in union with the divine life) and secondarily to quantity (*aiōnios*, "eternal," of infinite duration).

We have seen that for Paul immortality is a future acquisition, and all his references to eternal life (Rom 2:7; 5:21; 6:22–23; Gal 6:8; 1 Tim 1:16; 6:12; Titus 1:2; 3:7; cf. Acts 13:46; 1 Tim 4:8), apart from 1 Cor 3:22, seem to fall into this same category. The terms *immortal* and *immortality* are not found in the Synoptic Gospels where "eternal life" is reserved for the age to come (e.g., Mark 10:30), as in contemporary Jewish thought.

In the Fourth Gospel, too, eternal life sometimes denotes future blessing (e.g., John 4:14, 36; 5:29; 6:27; 12:25), but a distinctive feature of John's Gospel is the present dimension of eternal life (John 3:36; 5:24, 40; 6:47, 54; 12:49–50; cf. 1 John 2:24–25; 3:14–15; 5:11–13, 20). Here and now believers may in advance enjoy some of the blessings of the age to come. "Now this is eternal life: that they know you, the only true God, and Jesus Christ, whom you have sent" (John 17:3). Eternal life (or life) in John signifies (negatively) immunity from spiritual death (John 5:24) but not from physical death (John 11:25, "even though they die"), whereas for Paul immortality and eternal life involve immunity from both spiritual *and* physical death.

To relate Johannine eternal life with its present and future aspects to Pauline immortality with its negative side (immunity from decay and death) and its positive side (participation in the divine life), we may propose that eternal life is the positive aspect of immortality, and that immortality is the future aspect of eternal life.

H. *Relation between Immortality and Resurrection*

Here "resurrection" must refer to a "resurrection transformation" because believers alive at Christ's second coming will not be raised from death but will experience a transformation comparable to that of deceased Christians. As Paul expressed it, "We will not all sleep, but we will all be changed" (1 Cor 15:51).

What follows draws on material found in Harris, *Immortality*, 232–36, 239–40 (used with permission).

1. *They are inseparable ideas*

    a. Since the resurrection transformation of believers is the sole means of gaining immortality ("the dead will be raised immortal," 1 Cor 15:52), there can be no immortality without a prior resurrection transformation (Luke 20:35–36; Acts 13:34–35; Rom 6:9; 1 Cor 15:42, 52–54).

    b. Since immortality is the inevitable result of a resurrection transformation ("the dead will be raised immortal," 1 Cor 15:52), there can be no resurrection transformation without subsequent immortality (Luke 20:36b; John 11:25–26; Rom 6:9; 1 Cor 15:53–54; Rev 1:18; 20:6).

These two doctrines stand or fall together. Resurrection inevitably leads to immortality and immortality comes only through resurrection. To deny one is to deny the other. It is illegitimate to choose between the two, as if they were alternatives.

2. *They are complementary ideas*

    a. Resurrection prevents an *impersonal* view of immortality. Since believers will be raised to bear the image of "the man from heaven" (1 Cor 15:48–49) without

69

compromising their individuality, there is no place for an immortality of influence by which people live on in the abstract ideals they endorsed, or a familial immortality by which people live on in their posterity, or a pantheistic immortality in which individuals are absorbed into the universal divine life.

b. Resurrection forestalls an *individualistic* understanding of immortality. Believers are not destined for an individualized contemplative vision of God but for the corporate worship and service of God in the presence of all his people (1 Thess 4:17; Rev 7:13–15; 21:3; 22:3–4). Significantly, whenever a NT writer adds the qualification "of the dead" to the term *resurrection*, the word "dead" is always a plural (*nekroi*), never a singular.

c. The Christian doctrine of resurrection excludes any concept of immortality as a *disembodied* or purely spiritual existence. By his doctrine of the spiritual body (1 Cor 15:35–56), Paul was implicitly repudiating not only a materialistic view of resurrection (since it was a *spiritual* body) but also a spiritualistic view of immortality (since it was a spiritual *body*). Believers desire investiture with the spiritual body (2 Cor 5:2–4), not release from all embodiment.

Similarly, the NT doctrine of immortality clarifies the idea of resurrection.

a. Immortality guarantees that resurrection is seen not only as a spectacular event but also as an occurrence with equally dramatic consequences. Resurrection involves a *state* arising from an event. The person raised enjoys an immediate and permanent participation in the eternal divine life that guarantees incorruptibility and deathlessness.

b. Immortality guarantees the *permanency* of the resurrection state. Resurrection is no mere restoration of the dead to an unaltered physical life that therefore will once again end in death. Jesus is not only the Resurrection but also the Life. Once resurrected, Christians will permanently bear the image of God's Son (Rom 8:29; 1 Cor 15:49; 1 John 3:2).

c. Immortality guarantees the constant *invigoration* of the resurrected person. Just as the risen Christ "lives by the power of God" (2 Cor 13:4), so too the transformed follower of Christ will pulsate with perpetual divine energy (1 Cor 15:43).

I. *Comparison of Plato and Paul on Immortality*†

We shall compare a composite Pauline view drawn from the five of his letters where all of his references to immortality appear and a composite Platonic view that draws particularly on the *Phaedo* and the *Phaedrus*. Also see above (pages 3–4) for a summary of Plato's view of the tripartite soul. Plato was chosen for the comparison rather than any other ancient philosopher, not because the Platonic view of immortality was the dominant view in the ancient world, even among the Greeks, but because of the epochmaking significance of Plato's arguments for immortality in the history of ancient thought and their widespread influence among Christian thinkers. The evidence of Greek epitaphs shows, in fact, that the common person in Greece shared a Homeric rather than a Platonic view of what lay beyond the grave. One thinks of Achilles's piteous response to Odysseus: "Do not speak to me about death, renowned Odysseus. For I would rather be above on the earth, indentured to an insignificant man, than to be lord over all the dead" (*Odyssey* 11.498–99).

1. Paul portrays immortality as a natural property of God, and of God alone (1 Tim 6:16), so that creaturely beings gain immortality only through relationship with him. But for Plato

† This comparison is reproduced (with changes) from Harris, *Immortality*, 201–5 (used with permission).

immortality was an inherent characteristic of the rational "part" or function of the human soul because of its affinity with the invisible, eternal realm of Ideas or Forms and because of its participation in the Form of life.

2. In Platonic thought the individual person could lay claim to being immortal as a consequence of having a soul—the soul being tripartite (rational, spirited, appetitive). The immortality of a person's rational soul was an inherent and present possession, although only the true and unwavering philosopher could be said to be presently enjoying on earth the benefits of godlikeness (*Resp* 1.500D) and immortality (*Sym* 212A). But even when people prove themselves to be incurably guilty and so are condemned to eternal punishment in Tartarus, still the soul is not annihilated, for it never loses its natural property of immortality.

   In contrast, Paul depicts immortality as a future acquisition. Believers will be "raised immortal" (1 Cor 15:52), that is, will be raised and so become immortal, not raised as they already are, immortal. They will "put on" immortality (1 Cor 15:53–54). Whenever the two terms that may be translated "immortality"—*athanasia*, "undyingness," and *aphtharsia*, "indestructibility" (see pages 59–60 above)—are applied directly and personally to individuals (Rom 2:7; 1 Cor 15:52, 50, 52–54), the reference is always to a state that commences after death. Even those who equate immortality with eternal life and claim that the seed of immortality is implanted in the soul at the time of regeneration must concede the weight of this evidence and make the resurrection determinative for the full or the real possession of immortality.

3. Plato regards humans as composed of two parts. The soul is totally distinct from the body, being (in its rational form or function) eternally pre-existent, incorporeal, invisible, and indestructible. Allied, therefore, to Plato's view of psychical immortality is a negative view toward the body. The body is governed by sensation and by desire for pleasure (*Resp*

1.328D; 2.380E) and since it is a contaminating impedi-
ment to the attainment of truth (*Phaed* 66B), like a shell in
which an oyster is imprisoned (*Phaedr* 250C), it must be de-
nounced and despised (*Phaed* 65C, D). Admittedly, a more
positive view of the body occasionally emerges, especially in
Plato's later works, so that a correspondence is recognized
between bodily health and the wisdom of the soul (*Resp.*
3.404E; cf. 10.609C) and the body is seen as an instrument
of the soul (*Tim* 42.E, 43A), but it remains true that the
distinction between soul and body is not conceptual and
relative but real and absolute. Human beings are incarcerated souls. Death severs the chains of the body, emancipates
the soul, and makes possible pure intellectual knowledge
(*Phaed* 65A, 67A). Only the emancipation from corporeality brought by death enables the rational soul to re-enter its
true abode and breathe its natural air. Disembodiment is the
ideal state of the immortal soul.

Whether we regard Paul's anthropology as basically
monistic or decidedly dualistic, it cannot be said that he
views the human body as the temporary joining of a pre-
existent, immortal soul with a material, mortal body. Body
and soul are united in an organic union. The human individual is an "ensouled body," not an "embodied soul" or an
"incarcerated spirit." Humans are a psychosomatic unity, a
unified entity that relates to God and all creation by means
of a soul/spirit and a body. To the gathered Corinthians Paul
could say, "Although I (*egō*) am absent in body (*tō sōmati*) [=
not physically present], I am present in spirit (*tō pneumati*)"
(1 Cor 5:3; cf. Matt 10:28; 3 John 2). So far from being the
tomb or the tool of the soul, the body is a temple of the Holy
Spirit (1 Cor 6:19), a member of the corporate Christ (1 Cor
6:15), and a living sacrifice to God (Rom 12:1). This exalted
Pauline view of humans is consistent with his concept of death
and the afterlife. Death is not welcomed as release from embodiment, although it does terminate the pilgrimage of faith

(2 Cor 5:7–8) and inaugurate the vision of God (1 Cor 13:12). Spiritual embodiment is the ideal state of mortal beings.

4. It follows from Plato's repudiation of corporeality, both in the here and in the hereafter, that there is no room for the notion of the resurrection of dead persons.

   For Paul (and all the writers of the NT) there is no incompatibility between the ideas of immortality and resurrection (see above, pages 69–71). Immortality is gained through a resurrection transformation. And it is precisely this distinctive ingredient of resurrection that guarantees that immortality has a corporate as well as an individual dimension and relates to the whole person and not simply the soul.

5. Whereas Plato saw immortality as the property of all human souls, Paul regards it as conditional as well as being a future possession. According to Paul, it is death or a propensity to death, not immortality, that humankind inherits from Adam (Rom 5:12; 1 Cor 15:22), and it is "those who belong to Christ," not all who are "in Adam," who at Christ's coming will be made alive by a resurrection transformation that issues in immortality (1 Cor 15:22–23, 42, 52–54). Immortality is not a gift bequeathed to all by the first Adam but an inheritance won for the righteous by the second Adam (Christ). Possession of immortality is dependent on one's relation to the second Adam, not the first Adam.

6. In the case of Plato, the ultimate ground for the assurance of immortality was belief in the soul's divinity, belief in its affinity with transcendent Being. For Paul, and, we may assume, all the early Christians, the basis of confidence that they would inherit immortality was the gracious will of God, who already had given them his Spirit as a pledge of a transformation that would result in immortality (2 Cor 5:4–5) and had promised immortality for those who sought it by perseverance in well-doing (Rom 2:7).

So pronounced are these differences between the Pauline and Platonic concepts of immortality that it is easy to overlook certain similarities, although even here it is usually a case of "similarity with difference."

- In both cases, hope for immortality springs from a religious sentiment, although Plato is alone in enunciating philosophical arguments to buttress the intuition or belief.

- In each case belief in immortality is a stimulus to sound thinking and right action. Plato saw people's supreme goal as the care of their immortal soul, their real self, to ensure its happiness in the world beyond. Paul links eschatology and ethics as he moves directly from a discussion of the doctrine of immortality into an exhortation to be consistent and enthusiastic in the Lord's work (1 Cor 15:52–58).

- In Plato (*Phaed* 83E; *Resp* 10.613A; *Theaet* 176B), as in Paul, immortality involves "becoming like God," yet for the Christian this means conformity to the image of Christ (Rom 8:29; Col 3:10), rather than a "never-ending union with true reality," as in Plato.

- In both cases immortality is seen as personal, but in Plato immortality is "psychical" and incorporeal.

- Paul would agree with Plato that the earthly material body belongs to the world of mortality, but he would not agree that the body is alien to the soul and a dispensable element in real personhood.

The basic and irreconcilable differences between the views of Plato and Paul regarding immortality may be summarized this way.

	PLATO	PAUL
(i) immortality a natural product of . . .	the rational "part" of the soul	God alone
(ii) immortality regarded as . . .	a present possession	a future acquisition
(iii) ideal immortal state	disembodied	somatic
(iv) immortality associated with . . .	pure knowledge of Reality/ reincarnation	resurrection
(v) immortality the (future) possession of . . .	all human souls	"those who belong to Christ" (1 Cor 15:23)
(vi) assurance of immortality	belief in the soul's "divinity" (= affinity with transcendent Being)	possession of the Spirit as an *arrhabōn* ("pledge")

V. Eternity*

A. *Terminology*

The NT has no distinctive word for "eternity" but uses various combinations of the word *aiōn* ("age") to express this reality. In itself this word can refer to either a limited or an unlimited period of time, so that the common phrase *eis ton aiōna* has no uniform meaning and does not always mean "for [= throughout] the age [to come]" or "for ever." Its sense depends on the referent and the context.

- "Permanently/for a lifetime"—of a son's place in his family (John 8:35), and of the presence of the Spirit in believers (John 14:16)
- "To eternity/eternally" (BDAG 32b)/"for ever" (BDAG 289d):

    of Jesus's resurrected life (Heb 7:24)

    of Christ's priesthood (Heb 5:6; 6:20; 7:17)

    of the word of the Lord (1 Pet 1:25)

    of the believer's life (John 6:51, 58; 1 John 2:17)

    of the blessedness or praiseworthiness of God (Rom 1:25; 2 Cor 11:31) and of Christ (Rom 9:5)

    of the glory that belongs to God (Rom 11:36)

    of the future reign of Jesus (Luke 1:33)

* Material in this section is largely dependent on Harris, *Prepositions*, 94–97, 185 (used with permission).

There are three variations of this basic phrase, *eis ton aiōna* ("permanently," "eternally").

1. *Eis ton aiōna tou aiōnos* (lit. "for the age of age") means "for ever and ever" (only in Heb 1:8) (see #3 below).

2. *Eis tous aiōnas* (lit. "for the ages") is a plural form of the *eis ton aiōna*, where the plural may be generalizing or "Semitic" or simply a stylistic variation of the singular. Here the sense is "to all eternity" (BDAG 32b)/"eternally/for ever."

   • of the blessedness or praiseworthiness of God (Rom 1:25; 2 Cor 11:31) and of Christ (Rom 9:5)

   • of the glory that belongs to God (Rom 11:36)

   • of the future reign of Jesus (Luke 1:33)

3. The extended phrase *eis tous aiōnas tōn aiōnōn* (lit. "to the ages of ages") means "for ever and ever/for evermore" (BDAG 32b) and is a common formula in doxologies (Gal 1:5; Phil 4:20; 1 Tim 1:17; 2 Tim 4:18; Heb 13:21; 1 Pet 4:11; 5:11). It occurs thirteen times in Revelation. The added genitive "of ages" simply emphasizes the unendingness or eternality, but the two juxtaposed plurals suggest that from one perspective eternity may be considered an interminable accumulation of endless "ages."

Two other unique phrases must be noted. *Eis pantas tous aiōnas* (lit. "to all the ages," Jude 25) means "to all eternity" (BDAG 32b)/"for evermore"/"for ever and ever." Although *eis hēmeran aiōnos* in 2 Pet 3:18 could be rendered "until the day which is/of eternity" or "until the eternal day," more probably the sense is "until the day [of the Lord Jesus; cf. 2 Pet 3:10] that ushers in [future] eternity."

To express the notion of "eternity past," the preposition *pro* ("before") is used. Accordingly, we may render *pro pantos tou aiōnos* (lit. "before every age," Jude 25) by "before all time," or "before time began" (BDAG 32a), which is contrasted in this verse with *eis pantas tous aiōnas*, "to all eternity" (BDAG 32b). Similarly, *pro chronōn aiōniōn* (lit. "before eternal ages," 2 Tim 1:9; Titus 1:2) may be rendered "before the beginning of time," "from all eternity."

So, lacking one word for "eternity," the NT uses combinations with *aiōn* ("age") to capture the "tenses" of eternity past and eternity future. The point of orientation for any consideration of the past and future dimensions of eternity is the present time, "(right) now" (*nûn*, as is well illustrated by Jude 25: "to the only God, our Savior, is glory, majesty, power, and authority, through Jesus Christ our Lord, before time began (BDAG 32a) (= during eternity past), and now, and to all eternity (BDAG 32b) (= during eternity future)."

B. *Eternality of Christ in Hebrews*

Whether using one of the above phrases or equivalents, the author of Hebrews celebrates the eternality of Christ to an extent that is distinctive in the NT.

> "Your throne, O God, is for ever and ever" (Heb 1:8, citing Ps 45:6) not only affirms that Christ's dominion is everlasting; it also implies that the One occupying the throne is eternal.

> "You remain the same, and your years will never end." (Heb 1:12, citing Ps 102:27)

> As a priest in the eternal Melchizedekian order, Jesus would exercise his priesthood forever (Heb 5:6; 7:17, citing Ps 110:4; cf. Heb 6:20). Both the priesthood and the priest were eternal.

> One [Jesus] who has become a priest . . . on the basis of the power arising from an indestructible life. (Heb 7:16)

> Jesus lives forever . . . he has the power for all time (*eis to panteles*) to bring salvation to those who approach God through him, since he is always alive (*pantote zōn*) to plead on their behalf. (Heb 7:24–25)

"Jesus Christ, the same yesterday, today,—and for ever" (Heb 13:8). Although many church leaders may have modeled commendable lives of faith (Heb 13:7), they are no longer alive. By contrast, the immutable risen Jesus Christ personally embodies—forever—a perfect model to follow.

VI. Afterlife

Before the final form of the afterlife is experienced by humans, two divinely orchestrated events must take place—the return of Jesus to earth, and the final judgment of humans.

A. First Prelude: Second Advent of Jesus

1. Its nature

   Four nouns refer to this second advent, although sometimes verbs are used ("come (back)," John 14:3; 1 Cor 11:26; "appear," Col 3:4).

   a. *parousia* ("advent"), commonly used of a visit by a person of high rank, such as an emperor visiting a province, denotes the arrival of Christ on earth on a return visit (Matt 24:3, 27; 1 Cor 15:23; 1 Thess 4:15).

   b. *apokalypsis* ("unveiling," "revealing") refers to the full disclosure of Christ in his glory by the removal of everything that has hidden him from view (1 Cor 1:7; 2 Thess 1:7; 1 Pet 1:7, 13).

   c. *epiphaneia* ("appearing," "manifestation") describes the public and spectacular nature of Christ's appearing (2 Thess 2:8; 2 Tim 4:8).

d. *apantēsis* ("meeting") depicts the initial encounter between the triumphant Jesus and his resurrected followers (1 Thess 4:17).

The second advent is Christ's personal and visible return
to earth (Matt 24:27; 26:64; Acts 1:9–11; Rev 1:7), and therefore cannot be equated with a spiritual or "mystical" coming
of Christ in his church or its spread (note Acts 1:8) or with the
individual believer's death (note 1 Cor 15:23). At this future
advent Christ will have unsurpassed splendor and limitless
power and will be accompanied by his angels and saints (Matt
16:27; 25:31; 1 Thess 3:13; 4:14; 2 Thess 1:7).

This advent, sometimes called "the day (of the Lord/
God)" (e.g., 1 Thess 5:2, 4–5; 2 Pet 3:10, 12), marks the climax of God's personal intervention in human history. With
the first advent of Christ during "the present age" (Gal 1:4),
the age to come dawned (Heb 6:5; 9:26), but it has not yet
been consummated (1 Pet 4:7). Christians live in the "over-
lap" of the present age and the age to come (1 Cor 10:11).
Christ's second advent will mark the close of this age (Matt
24:3) and the full appearance of the age to come.

2. Its time

The return of Christ lies in the future (2 Pet 3:10), and so
cannot be identified as the coming of the Spirit, Jesus's other
Self (John 14:16–18), or with his "coming in judgment"
on Jerusalem in AD 70 (Matt 24:2, 15). It will be preceded
with signs (Matt 24:33; Luke 21:5–33; 2 Thess 2:3–4; 2 Tim
3:1–5) but the precise time of its occurrence is not known
by humans (Matt 24:36, 42; 25:13; Mark 13:32–33), so for
believers who are not ready for its arrival, its sudden and
unexpected occurrence may cause embarrassment (Matt
24:37–39, 42–44; Luke 21:34; 1 John 2:28).

The NT expression "the last days (or times)" refers not
only to the days immediately before the second advent of
Christ (as in 2 Tim 3:1; cf. 1 Tim 4:1), but also to all the days
after his first advent (Acts 2:16–17; Heb 1:1–2; 2 Pet 3:3–5;

Jude 18–19; cf. 1 Pet 1:20). Those living after the incarnation and Pentecost are permanently in "the last days" and therefore the End is perpetually near and may occur at any time. So we may speak of the "perpetual imminence" or "permanent impendingness" of Christ's second advent (cf. Phil 4:5; Jas 5:7–8; 1 Pet 4:7), not of its temporal proximity. Only if the parousia had been expected by the early church to occur within a specified period (such as the contemporary generation) can we legitimately speak of a "delay" in its arrival. The early Christians interpreted God's withholding of the End (? = "the 'delay' of the parousia") as a sign of his patience in permitting time for repentance (2 Pet 3:9).

3. Its sequel

   a. The judgment of the righteous and the unrighteous (see B. Second Prelude below).

   b. The resurrection of believers and of unbelievers (see above, pages 47–57).

   c. A reign of righteousness and peace in the "new heavens and new earth" (see below, pages 95–98).

4. Its present effect

   The second advent of Jesus is described as "the blessed hope" (Titus 2:13) because it brings a blessing after it occurs (see #3 above) and also before it happens (as below).

   a. It stimulates holy living (Rom 13:11–14; Col 3:4–5; Titus 2:12–13; 2 Pet 3:10–12; 1 John 3:2–3) and faithful, patient service (Matt 24:44–47; 1 Cor 15:57–58; Jas 5:7–8; 1 Pet 5:1–4).

   b. It promotes constant watchfulness (Mark 13:33, 36; Luke 21:34) and eager expectancy (Rom 8:19, 23; 2 Pet 3:12).

   c. It calms the anxious (John 14:1–3) and comforts the bereaved (1 Thess 4:13–18).

B. *Second Prelude: Divine Judgment*

In both Greek and English the term *judgment* has two basic senses: a judicial investigation that may lead to either a positive or a negative verdict; a negative verdict that involves some form of punishment.

Sometimes God the Father is said to be the judge (e.g., Rom 2:3, 5), sometimes Christ (e.g., 1 Cor 4:4–5). At other times, "the Lord's people" (1 Cor 6:2–3) or his "powerful angels" (2 Thess 1:7) are associated with him in his exercise of judgment.

But are there two separate tribunals before which humans must appear—"God's judgment seat" (*bēma*) (Rom 14:10) = "Christ's judgment seat" (*bēma*) (2 Cor 5:10), and God's "majestic and gleaming white throne" (*thronos*) (Rev 20:11)? There are clear similarities between the two tribunals: both assessments are conducted by God and Christ, who act in unison as joint occupiers of a single throne (Acts 10:42; 17:31; Rom 2:16; Rev 22:1, 3; cf. John 5:27); the assessments are individual ("each of us," 2 Cor 5:10; "each person," Rev 20:13) and reflect the assessors' full and accurate knowledge of a person's actions (Rom 2:6; Heb 4:12–13; cf. Jer 17:10). As for differences between the two tribunals, all believers will appear before the judgment seat of God or Christ (Rom 14:10; 2 Cor 5:10) and will receive "due recompense for actions, whether good or bad" (2 Cor 5:10) = divine praise or its forfeiture (1 Cor 3:14–15; 4:5; Col 3:24). On the other hand, "the rest of the dead" who were not part of the first resurrection (Rev 20:5), "the dead, great and small" (Rev 20:12), will appear before the great white throne. As those whose names were not found written in the book of life, they were thrown into the lake of fire (Rev 20:15).

Precisely when these final judgments will occur is unknown, but clearly they will follow Christ's second advent as the reigning Lord to whom all people are accountable (Phil 2:9–11; 2 Tim 4:1). But 2 Cor 5:8–10 and 2 Pet 2:9 (cf. Jude 6) indicate that at least a preliminary assessment of both believers and unbelievers occurs at their death.

The divine evaluation of believers is concerned with rewards for stewardship, not the determination of destiny. No longer trusting in "deeds (*erga*, plural) of the law" as the basis for justification (Rom 3:28), the Christian is nevertheless committed to "action (*ergon*, singular) stemming from faith" (1 Thess 1:3). So far from undermining the doctrine of justification by grace through faith, or from being a relic of Jewish belief unassimilated to the rest of Paul's teaching, the doctrine of judgment by works ensures that the justified sinner lives with a sense of moral earnestness and personal accountability. Nor are the notions of recompense and reward incompatible. Reward may be recompense for good actions; the "suffering of loss" (1 Cor 3:15), that is, the forfeiture of reward, may be requital for bad actions (cf. 2 Cor 5:10, "deeds whether good or bad"). Whatever else may be involved in the believer's reward at the divine judgment seat (1 Cor 9:25; 2 Tim 4:8; 1 Pet 5:4; Rev 2:10), an essential element in it is God's commendation (1 Cor 3:8; 4:5; cf. Rom 2:6, 10; 2 Cor 5:9), such as "Well done, good and trustworthy slave!" (Matt 25:21, 23)—commendation that may be given or withheld and may be given in varying measure ("At that time each person will receive their (due) praise from God," 1 Cor 4:5; "Each will be rewarded according to their own labor," 1 Cor 3:8).

In John 5:28–29 Jesus affirms that after all those in their graves hear his voice and come out, there will be two categories of people: "those who have done good deeds, to a resurrection that leads to life, and those who have done evil, to a resurrection that leads to judgment," or as the NIV renders it, "those who have done what is good will rise to live, and those who have done what is evil will rise to be condemned." This "resurrection that leads to condemnation" is clearly implied in Matt 5:29–30; 10:28; Rev 20:5, 11–15 and may possibly be inferred from Matt 12:41–42; 25:31–46; Luke 14:14; 20:35. The unrighteous dead will "rise up" and appear before God, either as disembodied spirits or in some undisclosed bodily form, and will be assessed on two bases: their relationship to Christ (Matt 7:22–23; 10:32–33; Mark 8:38; John 3:36; 2 Thess 1:8–9) and their works (Rom 2:6; 1 Pet 1:17; Rev

20:12–13). God will confirm the individual's prior decision regarding the claims of Christ, countersigning the check they have written throughout their lives.

1. Hades

Originally "Hades" was the name of the god of the lower or nether world, but it came to signify the place where all the departed dead go, "the realm of the dead" (Matt 11:23), so that Christ himself could be said to have been in Hades after his death (Acts 2:27, 31) and to have visited this realm to declare to fallen angels his complete victory over death and evil (on this controversial issue, see Harris, *Texts (2)*, 159–60). But Hades also refers to a place of torment (Luke 16:23), a citadel of death (Matt 16:18), or death personified (Rev 1:18; 6:8; 20:13–14). In these latter senses Hades came to be a synonym for hell in popular thought and expression.

2. Purgatory

In Roman Catholic thought purgatory is an interim state and place ("a waiting chamber for heaven") where some deceased believers, relying on God's grace, spend a limited time of penance to enable them to be purified from all traces of sin by gradual suffering and so become fit to be in God's presence in heaven.

Any NT passages appealed to in support of this view (such as 1 Cor 3:12; 2 Tim 1:18; or Rev 21:27) are irrelevant and unjustified. Basically, the idea that believers in Christ need further moral or spiritual refinement before being qualified to enter heaven flies in the face of a central message of the NT—that what we humans were unable to do to satisfy God's requirement of holiness (Rom 3:23) was successfully and fully accomplished by the Savior Jesus Christ when he reconciled us to God once and for all time by his substitutionary death (Rom 5:10; Heb 9:28; 1 Pet 2:24; 3:18), so that sacrifice (or penance) for sin is no longer necessary (Heb 10:18).

C. Final State of Believers

1. Heaven

The Greek term *ouranos* ("heaven") occurs in both singular and plural in the NT and corresponds to the Hebrew plural *šāmayim*. Linked with "earth" (*gē*) in the expression "heaven and earth" (e.g., Matt 5:18; Acts 4:24), it denotes the totality of creation. Contrasted with "earth," it refers to the sky above the earth (e.g., Acts 2:19, "heavens above . . . earth below"). Heaven is the dwelling place of angels (Matt 22:30) and of God (e.g., Deut 26:15; Matt 5:16, 45; 6:1, 9). Matthew's Gospel prefers "kingdom of heaven" over "kingdom of God," where "heaven" is an indirect reference to God, a reverent periphrasis, as in common Jewish practice. A sin against heaven (Luke 15:18, 21; cf. John 3:27) is a sin against God. When Jesus says he came down "from heaven" (John 3:13; 6:38, 42), he is saying he came "from the Father" (John 16:28). Sometimes the singular and plural of *ouranos* occur side by side with no apparent difference of meaning (e.g., Heb 9:23-24); Ephesians has only the plural while the Fourth Gospel has only the singular.

Conceived of as both a state and a locality, heaven contains all the elements of the Christian's "living hope" (1 Pet 1:3) or "blessed hope" (Titus 2:13).

- Worship and service of God and the Lamb (Rev 5:13; 22:3-4)
- Face-to-face fellowship with the risen Lord of the universe (1 Cor 13:12; 2 Cor 5:8; 1 Thess 4:17; Rev 22:4) (see above, page 25), perpetually witnessing his glory (2 Cor 3:18; 1 John 3:2; cf. Ps 17:15)
- Enjoyment of consummate, unending, and unsullied righteousness, peace, and joy (Rom 14:17; 2 Pet 3:13)
- Possession of a "spiritual body" that is perfectly adapted to the heavenly environment (1 Cor 15:42-44; 2 Cor 5:1-2) (see above, pages 48-51)

- Enrollment in "the Lamb's book of life" (Rev 13:8; 21:27; cf. Luke 10:20; Heb 12:23; Rev 3:5; 20:15)

- Enjoyment of reward (Matt 5:12; 16:27; Eph 6:8; Rev 22:12), treasures (Matt 6:20), and an unspoiled inheritance (Col 3:24; 1 Pet 1:4)

- Corporate fellowship with believers of all ages and of all generations in the city of God, the capital of the consummated kingdom (Rev 21:2–3)

- The permanent absence of sin (Rev 21:27), death, mourning, crying, and pain (Rev 21:4), hunger and thirst (Rev 7:16), and tears (Rev 7:17; 21:4)

In popular thought heaven is often considered to be a state of blissful inactivity and rest after the trials and tribulations of life on earth, or else a place of boring inaction. Nothing could be further from the NT's concept of life in "the new heaven and new earth" (on which see pages 88–90, 95–98 below).

a. Worship

Captivated by the majesty of divine beauty and power, the redeemed will become engrossed in ceaseless worship of God and the Lamb. If the unrighteous will be permanently excluded from the "majesty of the power of the Lord (Jesus)" (2 Thess 1:9), we may assume that the righteous will be accorded the privilege of witnessing that overwhelming majesty.

Revelation 4 depicts believers' worship of the Lord God as Creator (Rev 4:11):

> You are worthy, our Lord and God,
> to receive glory and honor and power,
> for you created all things,
> and by your will they were created
> and have their being.

Revelation 5 describes believers' worship of the Lamb as Redeemer (Rev 5:9, 12):

You are worthy to take the scroll
and to open its seals
because you were slain,
and with your blood you purchased for God
persons from every tribe and language and
people and nation.

Worthy is the Lamb, who was slain,
to receive power and wealth and wisdom and
strength
and honor and glory and praise!

Thus we move from the song of creation to the "new song" (Rev 5:9) of redemption. But Rev 5 ends (v. 13) with accolades given to joint recipients:

To him who sits on the throne and to the Lamb
be praise and honor and glory and power
for ever and ever!

b. Service

There is a sense in which "the dead who die in the Lord" permanently "rest from their labors" (Rev 14:13), but relief from toil does not amount to perpetual inactivity. The final state of believers will be one of joyful activity as they "follow the Lamb wherever he goes" (Rev 14:4). "For the Lamb at the center of the throne will be their shepherd; he will lead them to springs of living water" (Rev 7:17).

For various interpretations of the millennium (Rev 20:3–6), see Harris, *Texts (2)*, 170–72 where the three dominant views in Christian thought are outlined— postmillennialism, amillennialism, and premillennialism. To generalize, the Protestant Reformers rejected a purely symbolic view and regarded the thousand years as a variously defined past period of gospel success.

On the meaning of Paul's statement "All Israel will be saved," see Harris, *Texts (2)*, 62–63, where the three main identifications are mentioned and it is suggested that the reference is to ethnic Israel as a whole that is alive when the deliverer, Jesus, returns to earth from Zion, but not necessarily to every individual Jew.

The throne of God and of the Lamb will be in "the Holy City, the new Jerusalem" (Rev 21:2; 22:3) "and his slaves (*douloi*) will serve him" (Rev 22:3). It is not clear whether the singulars, "his" (*autou*) and "him" (*autō*), refer to the Lord God, to the Lamb (the nearest antecedent), or (more probably) to both regarded as forming an inviolate unity, just as in Rev 11:15 the one kingdom belongs to "our Lord" and "his Messiah," in Rev 21:22 the one temple in the heavenly city is "the Lord God Almighty and the Lamb," and in Rev 22:1 the one throne belongs to "God and the Lamb."

Whatever the precise nature of the devoted "service" performed, it is carried out by persons in willing servitude (*douloi*, "slaves") to a divine Master. It is a fascinating truth that the final biblical description of the eternal relationship between the redeemed and their Redeemer uses the slave-master metaphor (see further, Harris, *Slave, passim*). Their service includes being priests ("priests to serve," Rev 1:6; 5:10; cf. 20:6; 22:5). If the name that is inscribed on the foreheads of these slaves (Rev 22:4) is "holy to Yahweh" (LSB in Exod 28:36–38; Zech 14:20), the emphasis falls on the complete consecration ("holy") of these glorified believers in their service of God.

The final state of resurrected believers is permanent residence in the immediate presence of God and the Lamb, worshiping and serving them enthusiastically and acceptably for ever and ever in the new heaven and new earth, in spiritual bodies perfectly adapted to the new spectacular circumstances.

D. *Final State of Unbelievers*

Although the NT emphasizes the benefits of belief in God, it is unambiguous in declaring the dire consequences of ignoring or rejecting God's offer of forgiveness and new life as found in Christ (see above, pages 56–57). Nowhere is there a more incisive—and alarming—depiction of the eternal fate of unbelievers than in 2 Thess 1:7–9. As Paul assures the infant church in Thessalonica that God will repay their persecutors for their relentless persecution (2 Thess 1:6), he informs them that this divine retribution will occur "when the Lord Jesus is revealed from heaven in flaming fire along with his powerful angels, inflicting vengeance on those who do not know God and on those who do not obey the gospel of our Lord Jesus" (vv. 7b–8).

He continues, "These people will suffer the penalty of eternal destruction that involves being shut out from (*apo*) the presence of the Lord and from (*apo*) the majesty of his mighty strength, on the day he comes . . ." (v. 9).

This retribution is a destruction that is eternal. "Destruction" does not here refer to the act of destroying (as in 1 Cor 5:5) but to the state of ruin (as also in 1 Thess 5:3). When the adjective *aiōnios* ("eternal") describes God (as in Rom 16:26), it signifies "without beginning or end"; when used of past time (as in Rom 16:25), the meaning is "long ago"; in describing other entities such as *olethros* ("destruction") here, the sense is "with a beginning but without an end," that is, "of unending duration." In its essence, the ruin that is destined to last for ever is permanent exclusion from the presence of the One who is the ultimate source of consummate pleasure, and also from the incomprehensible delight of witnessing his majestic power. To become aware of this irreversible deprivation will cause the spiritual torment, despair, and loneliness associated with "the outer darkness," "the blazing furnace," and "weeping and gnashing of teeth" referred to by Jesus on several occasions (Matt 8:12; 13:41–42, 50; 22:13; 25:30, 41; Luke 13:28; cf. 2 Pet 2:17; Jude 7).

1. Gehenna

"Gehenna" (*geenna*) is the Greek form of the Hebrew *gē-hinnōm*, "Valley of Hinnom" (Josh 15:8; 18:16), that was a ravine south of Jerusalem associated with Israelite idolatry and child sacrifice (2 Kgs 23:10; 2 Chr 28:3; 33:6; Jer 7:31; 19:1–5). It became a dumping ground for corpses and ashes (Jer 31:40). Being linked with death, fire, and judgment (cf. Isa 66:24), it symbolized a place of punishment for sinners and became synonymous with hell (Matt 23:33, "sentenced to Gehenna," or "sentenced to hell," NRSV).

2. Hell

In modern English usage the word *hell* has two basic senses (that correspond to the two uses of Hades): the abode of the dead; and (the predominant use) a place or state of pain or misery for the wicked (as in the dismissive imprecation "Go to hell!"). On the phrase "[Christ] descended into hell" found in the Apostles' Creed, see Harris, *Texts (2)*, 159–60 (which deals with 1 Pet 3:18b–19; 4:6) where a defensible view is proposed that after Jesus's resurrection and as part of his ascension to heaven, he visited the realm of the dead and declared to the host of fallen angels his complete victory over death and evil. Such an interpretation of Christ's "descent into hell" would accord with Peter's desire to reassure his readers/hearers that in the divine plan vindication follows innocent suffering.

3. Conditional Immortality and Annihilationism

We have seen that the receipt of immortality is conditional in the sense that only "those who belong to Christ" by embracing the gospel will receive God's gift of immortality. This is radically different from a popular view that posits the annihilation of the unrighteous by divine fiat as the corollary of "conditional immortality": the righteous become immortal but the unrighteous perish by "the fire that consumes," with or without prior punishment. On this view, the ultimate punishment is "eternal" in the sense that its results are irreversible, not that it continues for ever. Everlasting torment is purely vindictive or retributive and incompatible with a compassionate loving God. In addition, if in fact in the end there is eternal bliss in heaven alongside eternal suffering in hell, we are left (it is claimed) with a permanent cosmic dualism that is incompatible with the universal sovereignty of God.

With regard to those NT passages where the punishment of unbelievers is described as "eternal" (Matt 25:46; 2 Thess 2:9), it is inadequate to claim that the adjective *aiōnios* means "aeonial" or "belonging to the Age to come," so that the punishment takes place *in* eternity rather than lasting *throughout* eternity. In Matt 25:46 the precise parallelism ("they [the unrighteous] will go away to eternal punishment, but the righteous to eternal life") shows that the one adjective *aiōnios*, used twice, must bear the same meaning with "punishment" as it does with "life"—"of everlasting duration." Similarly in 2 Thess 1:9 the loss involved in being permanently banished from God is not only inestimable (it is "ruin," *olethros*) but also irreversible in its nature, not only in its results (it is "eternal ruin," *olethros aiōnios*). If the essence of heaven is the exhilarating presence of God, the essence of hell is the devastating absence of God.

Neither the OT nor the NT envisions the possibility of the total extinction of persons, as attractive as this concept may be in comparison with the notion of unending torment of spirit. That the verb "perish" (*apollusthai*) does not imply annihilation is clear from its use in John 11:50; Acts 5:37; 1 Cor 10:9–10; Jude 11, and from the occurrence of its present tense, "those who are perishing" (*hoi apollumenoi*) in 1 Cor 1:18 and 2 Cor 2:15. Just as God was sovereign in his loving decision to give humans freedom of choice, so he is sovereign in his loving decision to confirm the consequences of their choice. His holiness reigns supreme, being central in God's love: death and Hades will be thrown into the lake of fire, along with those whose names are not found written in the book of life (Rev 20:14–15). Also, when Jesus describes God as "the One who can destroy both soul and body in Gehenna" (Matt 10:28; most EVV have "in hell"), the indication of location ("in Gehenna") would be irrelevant if "soul and body" were annihilated.

4. Universalism

Some defenders of the view that in the end all people will enjoy God's salvation appeal to general theological arguments to support their position. If God was pleased to reconcile all things to himself (Col 1:18–19) so that at the End he is "all in all" (1 Cor 15:28), how can any of his human creatures fall outside that divinely ordered universal restoration? Moreover, if humans have the power to resist God's love eternally, does that not call into question his omnipotence? Will not God's desire for everyone to be saved and to come to a knowledge of the truth (1 Tim 2:4) be eternally frustrated if many of his creatures resist him forever in hell?

Other universalists point to many NT passages (such as the following) that speak of salvation where "all" seems to mean "everybody."

- "God has bound everyone over to disobedience so that he might be merciful to *all*" (Rom 11:32).
- "As in Adam all die, so in Christ *all* will be made alive" (1 Cor 15:22).
- "For the grace of God has appeared, bringing salvation to *all people*" (Titus 2:11).

In all such proof texts for universalism the immediate or wider context of the verse cited is often overlooked. For example, in 1 Cor 15:22 the "all" in the phrase "in Christ all will be made alive" is immediately restricted in the next verse (v. 23) to "those who belong to him." Or again, God's mercy extended to all (Rom 11:32) has to be understood

94

in light of Paul's earlier distinction between those who will be given eternal life and those who will face God's wrath and anger (Rom 2:7-8). Context usually shows that "all" refers to "all without distinction" (whether Jew or gentile, male or female, slave or free), not "all without exception." On the other side, there are many places in the NT where "salvation" is clearly restricted to the followers of Jesus (e.g., Matt 25:34, 41, 46; John 3:36; 5:24, 29; Rom 2:7-8; 2 Thess 1:8-10) and no places where the prospect is envisaged of people's destiny being altered after death.

On the wider issues, it would be improper for a God who had entrusted all people with the inalienable right to make their own choices to override that freedom by forcing their ultimate submission to his will. There are self-imposed limits to his omnipotence. If the essence of salvation is coming to a knowledge of the truth (1 Tim 2:4), it must remain an option for individuals to reject that advance and so remain remote from that salvation. Forced submission to God would convert heaven into an agonizing hell for those who died in open rebellion to God.

E. *New Heavens and New Earth*

Two NT passages speak of "a new heaven/new heavens and a new earth." In one case the "newness" seems to occur after a prior conflagration; in the other case, it seems to result from a transformation.

1. 2 Peter 3:12b-13

"That day [the day of God, v. 12a] will cause the heavens to be dissolved by fire and the elements to melt in fervent heat. But in keeping with his promise we are waiting for new heavens (*ouranous*, plural) and a new earth, where righteousness finds it home."

The preceding verses (vv. 7 and 10) also speak of complete annihilation: "the present heavens (*hoi nun ouranoi*, plural) and earth have been reserved for fire ..." (v. 7); "The heavens (*ouranoi*, plural) will disappear with a whirlwind roar (*hroizēdon*); the elements (= heavenly bodies) will be dissolved by fire; and the earth and everything that was done on it will be exposed" (v. 10). This would seem to correspond to God's future "once and for all" (*hapax*) "shaking" of not only earth but also heaven (Heb 12:26) which is explained in the next verse (Heb 12:27) as "the removal of what is shaken—that is, created things—so that what cannot be shaken may remain." Also, replacement after removal appears to be implied in Isa 65:17, "See, I will create new heavens and a new earth. The former things will not be remembered, nor will they come to mind."

2. Revelation 21:1, 5

> I saw a new heaven and a new earth, for the first heaven and the first earth had disappeared, and there was no longer any sea . . . . He who was seated on the throne said, "I am making everything new."

The Greek word *kainos* ("new") (used twice in 2 Pet 3:13 and three times in Rev 21:1, 5) describes something that replaces what has become obsolete (the first heaven and the first earth); it is "new" in the sense of "not previously known" and is superior in kind to the old (see BDAG 497a–b). After the disappearance of the first heaven and the first earth, there is not a second heaven and second earth of the same kind, but a heaven and earth previously unknown.

Alongside the above references to the replacement of the present universe are NT passages that refer to a recreation or reconstitution of the universe through renewal. Jesus promised his disciples that they would share with him his coming role as judge "when all things are renewed" (*en tē palingenesia*, literally, "in the rebirth") (Matt 19:28). That is, the universe will "again (*palin*) come to be (*ginesthai*)" what it originally was. It is relevant that in the only other NT use of *palingenesia*, the term is associated with a word that means "renewal" (*anakainōsis*, Titus 3:5). The renewal of the believer (Titus 3:5) anticipates the regeneration of the universe (Matt 19:28). Peter too speaks of the "restoration" (*apokatastasis*) of the physical world to its original purity and perfection that was promised by the prophets (Acts 3:21; cf. Isa 65:17). In Rom 8:19–22 Paul indicates that creation's destiny is liberation from its frustration (v. 20) and bondage to decay (v. 21), not annihilation.

How, then, are we to reconcile these disparate notions of annihilation followed by replacement, and transformation of what already exists? One way is to propose that fire may be seen as an agent of purification, so that 2 Pet 3 is describing the rejuvenation of the universe, not its total destruction. But it is difficult not to interpret "dissolution" or "melting" or "disappearance" as indicators of extinction.

An alternative (and preferable) way is to suggest that the ideas of exchange and change, replacement and renewal, are simply complementary or alternative ways of envisaging a reality (revolution), just as Paul can speak of the resurrection body as replacing the physical body (2 Cor 5:1; cf. 1 Cor 15:44) but also of putting on the new body over the old (2 Cor 5:4; cf. 1 Cor 15:53–54). These *sui generis* revolutions are ultimately beyond human understanding.

In whatever way the "new earth" comes into existence, one crucial aspect of its "newness" will be the permanent absence of the detrimental effects of human sin alongside the regaining of its pristine purity. Similarly, the "new heaven(s)" will be "new" in that "nothing impure will ever enter it" (Rev 21:27) as had happened before when Satan and his demonic minions (2 Cor 11:14–15) inhabited the precincts of heaven (Job 1:6–12; 2:1–7; Zech 3:1–2; Luke 10:18) before they are cast into the eternal fire (Matt 25:41; Rev 20:10).

Some have suggested that heaven and earth, being renewed, will be integrated with each other. But clearly the new earth has not become the new heaven, for when John expands on his vision by saying "I saw the Holy City, the new Jerusalem, coming down out of heaven from God" (Rev 21:2), he must be referring to the new heaven, where God still resides ("from God"; cf. Ezek 66:22), since the first heaven had disappeared (Rev 21:1). Deceased believers who had been in Christ's (and God's) presence in heaven since their death (Luke 23:43; 2 Cor 5:8; Phil 1:23; see above, pages 24-25) will now have been joined by believers who were alive at Christ's advent (1 Thess 4:17). How God can remain enthroned in the new heaven ("a loud voice from the throne," Rev 21:3) but simultaneously have his dwelling place among his redeemed people on the new earth (Rev 21:3) might seem a mystery, but one of God's qualities is his omnipresence.

All NT writers share the conviction that what people believe about human destiny influences their attitudes and conduct (e.g., Matt 24:42-44; 25:13; Mark 13:32-37; Luke 16:9; John 14:1-3; 1 Cor 15:58; Heb 11:9-10; Jas 5:8; 1 Pet 1:13, 17; 1 John 3:2-3; Jude 17-23). Eager expectation for "the day of the Lord" prompts purity of life (2 Pet 3:11-14). Eschatology is linked with ethics. The glimpses of the future afforded by the NT are designed to stimulate holy living, not to satisfy idle curiosity about the future. "All who have this hope in Christ purify themselves, just as he is pure" (1 John 3:3).

Also, if from a human perspective there seems to be a delay in God's fulfillment of his promise to create a heaven and earth that are without precedent and superior to their predecessors, it is because of his patient desire to bring everyone to repentance (2 Pet 3:8-9).

In its essence, the Christian hope focuses not on a series of spectacular events but on a person, the Lord Jesus Christ, who will set in motion and superintend the series of events that will herald the arrival of the consummated kingdom of God (Phil 3:20-21). A right relationship with the Last One (Rev 22:13) and complete devotion to his service (1 Cor 15:58) are infinitely more important than having an imagined impeccable chronology of the last things.

Bibliography

Alcorn, Randy. *Heaven.* Carol Stream, IL: Tyndale, 2004.

Alexander, T. D. *From Eden to the New Jerusalem: Exploring God's Plan for Life on Earth.* Nottingham, UK: InterVarsity, 2008.

Barr, James. *The Garden of Eden and the Hope of Immortality.* Oxford: Oxford University Press, 1993.

Bauckham, Richard. *The Fate of the Dead: Studies on the Jewish and Christian Apocalypses.* Leiden: Brill, 1998.

Benoit, Pierre, and Roland E. Murphy, eds. *Immortality and Resurrection.* New York: Herder, 1970.

Brower, Kent E., and Mark W. Elliott, eds. *"The Reader Must Understand": Eschatology in Bible and Theology.* Leicester, UK: Apollos, 1997.

Cavallin, H. C. C. *Life after Death: Paul's Argument for the Resurrection of the Dead in 1 Corinthians 15.* Lund: Gleerup, 1974.

Charlesworth, J. H., et al., eds. *Resurrection: The Origin and Future of a Biblical Doctrine.* London: T&T Clark, 2006.

Clark-Soles, J. *Death and the Afterlife in the New Testament.* London: T&T Clark, 2006.

Cooper, J. W. *Body, Soul and Life Everlasting: Biblical Anthropology and the Monism–Dualism Debate.* Grand Rapids: Eerdmans, 2000.

Cullmann, Oscar. *Immortality of the Soul or Resurrection of the Dead?* London: Epworth, 1958.

Darragh, J. T. *The Resurrection of the Flesh.* New York: Macmillan, 1921.

Duthie, C. S., ed. *Resurrection and Immortality.* London: Bagster, 1979.

Finney, M. T. *Resurrection, Hell and the Afterlife: Body and Soul in Antiquity, Judaism and Early Christianity.* London: Routledge, 2016.

Fudge, E. W. *The Fire That Consumes: The Biblical Case for Conditional Immortality.* Rev. ed. Milton Keynes, UK: Paternoster, 2005.

———. *The Fire That Consumes: A Biblical and Historical Study of the Doctrine of Final Punishment.* 3rd ed. Eugene, OR: Cascade, 2011.

Gowan, D. E. *Eschatology in the Old Testament.* 2nd ed. Edinburgh: T&T Clark, 2000.

Green, Joel B. *Body, Soul and Human Life: The Nature of Humanity in the Bible.* Milton Keynes, UK: Paternoster, 2008.

Hallote, R. S. *Death, Burial, and Afterlife in the Biblical World: How the Israelites and Their Neighbors Treated the Dead.* Chicago: Dee, 2001.

Harris, Murray J. *From Grave to Glory: Resurrection in the New Testament.* Grand Rapids: Zondervan, 1990.

————. *Raised Immortal: Resurrection and Immortality in the New Testament.* Grand Rapids: Eerdmans, 1985.

Hilborn, David, ed. *The Nature of Hell: A Report by the Evangelical Commission on Unity and Truth among Evangelicals.* Carlisle, UK: Paternoster, 2000.

Hoekema, A. A. *The Bible and the Future.* Grand Rapids: Eerdmans, 1979.

Jersak, Bradley. *Her Gates Will Never Be Shut: Hope, Hell, and the New Jerusalem.* Eugene, OR: Wipf & Stock, 2009.

Johnston, P. S. *Shades of Sheol: Death and the Afterlife in the Old Testament.* Leicester, UK: Apollos, 2002.

Longenecker, Richard N., ed. *Life in the Face of Death: The Resurrection Message of the New Testament.* Grand Rapids: Eerdmans, 1998.

MacDonald, Gregory [a.k.a. Robin A. Parry]. *The Evangelical Universalist: The Biblical Hope That God's Love Will Save Us All.* 2nd ed. Eugene, OR: Cascade, 2012.

Middleton, J. R. *A New Heaven and a New Earth: Reclaiming Biblical Eschatology.* Grand Rapids: Baker, 2014.

Moo, Jonathan, and Robin Routledge, eds. *As Long as the Earth Endures: The Bible, Creation and the Environment.* Nottingham, UK: Apollos, 2014.

Morgan, C. W., and R. A. Peterson, eds. *Heaven.* Wheaton, IL: Crossway, 2014.

Neusner, J., ed. *Death and the Afterlife.* Eugene, OR: Wipf & Stock, 2000.

Nichols, T. *Death and the Afterlife: A Theological Introduction.* Grand Rapids: Brazos, 2010.

Oyen, G. van, and T. Shepherd, eds. *Resurrection of the Dead: Biblical Traditions in Dialogue.* Leuven: Peeters, 2012.

Powys, David. *"Hell": A Hard Look at a Hard Question: The Fate of the Unrighteous in New Testament Thought.* Carlisle, UK: Paternoster, 1997.

Segal, Alan. *Life after Death: The History of the Afterlife in Western Tradition.* New York: Doubleday, 2014.

Smith, J. K. *Dust or Dew? Immortality in the Ancient Near East and in Psalm 49.* Eugene, OR: Pickwick, 2011.

Sprinkle, Preston M., ed. *Four Views on Hell.* Counterpoints. Grand Rapids: Zondervan, 2016.

Stendahl, Krister, ed. *Immortality and Resurrection.* New York: Macmillan, 1965.

Williamson, P. R. *Death and the Afterlife: Biblical Perspectives on Ultimate Questions.* Downers Grove, IL: InterVarsity, 2017.

Witherington, Ben. *Jesus, Paul and the End of the World: A Comparative Study in New Testament Eschatology.* Exeter, UK: Paternoster, 1992.

Wright, Tom. *New Heaven, New Earth: The Biblical Picture of Christian Hope.* Cambridge: Grove, 1999.

www.ingramcontent.com/pod-product-compliance
Lightning Source LLC
Chambersburg PA
CBHW020207090426

42734CB00008B/972